T0128106

You and Me Getting Under Limbo Bars

Howard Seeman, Ph.D.

authorHOUSE®

AuthorHouse™
1663 Liberty Drive
Bloomington, IN 47403
www.authorhouse.com
Phone: 1 (800) 839-8640

Published by AuthorHouse   05/09/2018

ISBN: 978-1-5462-3666-5 (sc)
ISBN: 978-1-5462-3667-2 (e)

DEDICATION
to
Robert W. Siroka, Ph.D.

For helping me find and grow the "flashlight" now inside me that is able to find and identify these feelings, then to feel unalone about them, to feel safe to express them. Thus, many others wonderfully get this tool as well, from me, from you. I thank you with love and appreciation [that you went through your own pain, learning and work to give this] and *a thank you* also from the *many others* we have given to, through you.

Love,

Howard

Preface

You and me - we must climb out of our childhood and get under the many *limbo bars* that can hurt our growing, our ability to rise up from many painful past events, realizations, losses... .

Come and read my memoirs on growing. They are yours too; you are not alone. We have gone through similar events and feelings. Come, let's understand them better together, so we can grow more, more aware, and thus have more *life*.

Such gives us our own appreciation for how well we have done, for how far we have gotten.

Warm regards,

Howard

Contents

1. This is where I started

I'm eight years old. It's Saturday and my mother, annoyed from ironing, cleaning, cooking, always anxious my father will be annoyed…, tells me: "Why don't you go downstairs and play with the other kids?" with the tone: "Why don't you get out of my hair?" It's only 9:00 am. No one will be downstairs on the street to play with, but I have to go downstairs.

I open the door to the apt. and go out onto my 6th floor hallway of my building in the Bronx. The hallway is empty. I push the button for the elevator. Waiting for the elevator, the hallway is dark and scary; I hope the elevator comes soon. It comes, it's empty. I get in and push: #1 to the lobby, and I walk out the front of the building through a big steel gate onto the street.

I look up and down the street. No one is on the street: only parked cars, concrete sidewalks, buildings, and buildings. An empty block.

A car suddenly goes by. Then, emptiness again.

I try to figure out what to do? But no kids are around yet, so I sit down on the steps of the building. All the way at the end of the street I can see the top of the Empire State Building; it's way off in what my teacher told me is Manhattan. The sun is rising, but I can't see it rise. It is somewhere behind these six story buildings. I will eventually see the sun about 1 o'clock, but only peering out over one of these buildings. I will have to wait till I am 26 years old (a woman I will date will take me to the cliffs of Cape Cod. There I will finally see the sun rise.)

Another car goes by.

No one is still out yet. I sit on the cold stoop with nothing to do. I wish it wasn't so quiet. I'm supposedly in the state of New York, in the United States. Supposedly there are other kids in other countries too, like China, and Egypt … Maybe some are playing ball?

They say that I'm in the largest city on the Earth. But, the Earth is just a moving rock in space? The Earth really doesn't have a name? We named it? The other nearest rock I can see we call the moon; they say it is 280,000 miles away.

Another car goes by.

At night, if I sneak up onto my roof, I can see the lights of Manhattan, and millions of stars that are supposedly like our sun. My roof is scary; no one is up there at night. Supposedly all these stars I see are in this thing called our galaxy, called the Milky Way. Supposedly the sun goes down every night and shines on China.

This Milky Way is supposedly so large they tell me that even if I traveled the speed of light, 186,000 miles a second, it would still take me like a 100,000 years to get out of it.

I wonder if anybody out there really can hear me? Out there my parents would be gone, my sister, my dog, all the kids on my block.

For now, I am here.

Another car goes by.

Still no one on my block yet. Years from now I will be 75 years old.

Ah, here comes Irwin. We'll tell "knock-knock jokes", or something like that, or play hide-and-go-seek when enough kids come down. Irwin is seven; he and I didn't know it then, but he will die of cancer when he is 14.

Irwin sits down next to me and says, "Hi, how are you?" and smiles. I say, "OK."

Another car goes by.

2. My first encounter with dying

I was 6 years old. My father let me have a fish tank; he even helped me with it. A good job? I had to change the water, pick out fish, feed them, sometimes empty the tank, clean it, sometimes there was a leak. My first working job.

One day, while doing these jobs, I noticed something strange in the tank: one of the fishes was swimming upside down. At first I thought, "Wow, that's not easy." I grabbed the fish net and decided to poke it to tell it to stop doing that. It did not object. No matter how much I poked it, it did not object. Strange I thought: all other people, things, dogs... they object. I poked it harder. It just laid there. That got me: it just laid there. Now, I felt bad for it. I wanted to help it move. I tried: "Move!" and poked it harder, then carefully, gently, tried dropping food near it. It still did not move.

Now in my 70s, if I go to the beach at night and look up at the sky, or watch my fellow humans...I remember this. The fish had died. It had died. I now know the meaning of this well, too well.

I eventually walked away from the fish tank, into my bedroom and lied down. I looked at the ceiling, and then sucked my thumb. Eventually my mother called me. So I got up. But actually, I have never gotten up, completely.

I decided to walk thru many mazes, past trees, drive cars, ride bikes, eat at restaurants, go to college, work, listen to my friends. On and on.

When I was 15 years old, we moved out of the city; I left my block that I had grown up on since I was a week old. Doing: blocks, checkers, monopoly, TV with my sister, stick ball, playing catch, trying to <u>not</u> be afraid of girls....

We moved up to a small town near Peekskill; I went to a high school there. One day, I got a letter from my friend on my old block: Jeffrey. He wrote me that Irwin had died. Irwin had died. I thought: that was impossible! Irwin was only 13, he hid behind parked cars well during Hidin&GoSeek, could bite his own toe nails, had a great mother, never hurt anybody. I could not believe that Irwin had died, was gone.

I still do not believe it.

I had a dog named Major. He knew me better than anyone. He listened to me better than anyone.

Why did his back legs start to hurt? Why did my sister [after he was about 10] have to take him to the Vet., and not come out with Major?

Why can't my dear Ros fight her way back from dying? She was such a great fighter.

I don't like it that the sun goes down every day.

When I was sixteen I pleaded with my father to have a BB gun. He finally relented and got me one. I assembled it, and saw out my country house window: a little rabbit. I aimed at the little rabbit as it ran across the lawn. It stopped; I missed? I pulled the trigger again. It still stopped. I shot again. It still would not move. I went outside and slowly, not to scare it, approached the little bunny. It had 3 holes in it.

Then, when I was 35, there was Danny and I.

Danny [I called him *DaniEL*; he called me *Fats*] was great at tennis player; we did bowling, billiards, Frisbee, basketball... However, since he was so tall, when he was on ice-skates, he was a riot. His center of gravity was up around his shoulders; he was like a wobbly shmoo, and we laughed our heads off every time he would wobble and slowly try to not fall down; but he did. A riot.

We saw Dr. Ahmed, his oncologist together, many times, going over his x-rays, treatments, waiting for the results many, many times. I sat in waiting rooms looking at magazines. Waiting. Once I asked Dr. Ahmed: "How will we know when Danny is cured of this cancer?" Dr. Ahmed said, "When he dies of something else."

I wanted to play with DaniEL forever, but we did not even make it to checkers.

4

Santa, please take death away.

Superman, please kill it.

Mom, please?

I sometimes go to the beach at night alone and look up at the stars. I now know that there are billions of stars up there, just in our galaxy, and there are billions and billions of galaxies. Then I feel the privilege of being alive, that I am lit up for such a short time…while with friends laughing or when at funerals, or just watching dear fragile friends [secretly], or watching children, trees, flowers.

I now take care of many plants in my Apt. I water them, some leaves die, I trim them, I do cuttings and grow more. I like them and I get satisfaction from taking care of them. A job? Yes. It is my old fish tank.

3. Family

Sitting at dinner with my unhappy sister, my mother still cooking, my father telling me "don't", and then him complaining to my mother about his asshole bosses... was my family. Walking away into rooms where they were not, was always calmer. However, I could still hear the yelling. My sister, very needy, cried and cried when we were fighting, and thus won.

My mother was always saying: "What?! What do you want now?!" My father: "Leave your mother alone!" ["She's for me!" was what I heard.]

"Mommy, can you play with me?" I was 5, very alone-bored; she was ironing, ironing, ...then dishes, then cooking, then always worried about something. "Mommy can you play with me, a little?"

My mother: "Go bang your head against the wall!"

Years later, in school, this teacher [her name will always be in my care]: Mrs. Morris, chewed gum with a slight smile, and sat at the piano and taught us songs. Then we'd sing... like: "Ride the Chariot in the Morning", that we were going to perform in the auditorium on... Dec. 20.   Then came Dec. 20.

We were able, I was able, to march onto that big school stage, all one hundred of us, facing my whole school packed auditorium. Then wonderful Mrs. Morris slowly walked out and got up in front of us - the chorus she had molded for weeks –and then turned her back to the audience and looked only at us. We were alone with her; she smiled at us, then winked at us. She loved us. We loved her.

Then, with that smile, she raised her arms high, held them up in the air, looked into our eyes, and winked at us that: "ready, here we go!" wink. Then with one powerful downward stroke of her arms, all one hundred of us sang together one great rainbow chord.

That was my first real experience of family.

4. Realizing time and my dad

When I was seven years old, I noticed something in 5 seconds that changed my whole life.

I thought my father was evil.

Screaming at me, he would pull off his belt and whip me with it. My mother was reluctant to protect me.

He would also place charts on the kitchen wall for the whole family to see - marking every time I sucked my thumb. One time, he put iodine on my thumb and told me: "If you suck your thumb, you will die."

When I would hear the door open when he was coming home from work, the whole apt. would suddenly get scary.

I was seven years old one summer when he decided we would all go to the country for two weeks for a family vacation. It sounded wonderful. But, after we got there, my father informed me that it was best that I go to "sleep away" camp. I was sent away, banished to a what felt like a *prison camp*. I cried, and cried…. then held it in. Worse: my younger sister could stay and have my Mom and Dad to herself. I was thrown, packed, encased into a bus, and sent away.

Camp for me was hell. I lived there holding my breath for two weeks. Worse: I wet the bed every night. To not be embarrassed every morning, I would get up secretly about 3am and sneak out alone onto the dark night bunk porch, [dark mountains surrounded everything] and try to dry my wet sheets before they woke up to find out: "He wet the bed."

I hated hearing that trumpet playing on that scratchy record every morning across empty fields. Then, having to line up, always a little afraid to stand next to anybody. I was a lost, orphan in empty mountains. I remember pleading with my parents in postcards: "Please send me comic books." All the other boys had comic books. They never did.

Finally, they put us onto the buses to go home. Depleted from constant depression, I rode the camp bus home in the back - while all the other kids sang camp songs.

Then, it happened:

The bus pulled into the bus depot; hundreds of parents were there waiting to get their kids. Then, I saw my father.

He was in a frenzy trying to find me. He kept yelling to my mother, "Where, where!? I don't see him!" "Over there Al." she kept saying, trying to calm and soothe him. "Where, where?!" he kept yelling.

My father looked scared, weak, and lost, and he needed my mother. I suddenly noticed for the first time in my life that my father was getting old, and that he was only 28.

In those 5 seconds I noticed: Time, and the entire breath of my life.

And, that my father was not evil.

5. A simple trauma

"Howard, you're making a big deal out of this!"

"Dad, I know you died many years ago, but please don't still yell at me."

"I know this happened to me over 64 years ago, and it seems like no big deal to you, maybe even funny to you, but it upset me sooo. I still feel the sting of it. I wish I could take it out of my life. Just try to understand…. please?"

"Ok Howard, but this is ridiculous. Tell you what: You can tell it to the jury, you can tell your heart out to them, and see what they think. Ok? But, this is really a waste of time."

"Ok".

"Ok, begin!"

I was 10 years old. I loved Audrey. She was beautiful. I would get very scared if she was coming down the block towards me, even if she was with friends. She was always laughing. I wish I could do that. When she got close, I kinda shrunk. I wished I was a turtle and could tuck my head in. After she passed by, I would try to look at her, of course hoping she would not see me looking at her. She was beautiful. For hours after seeing her, I could not stop thinking about her.

Then, this horrible, terrible, painful thing happened.

I was on the other side of the street, just walking, I think to school. But, I had to pee very badly. I was afraid I would not make it to a bathroom; the kids would then see I wet my pants. So, I looked everywhere, but I could only find just parked cars. I had to go very badly. So, I took out my little penis, looked around and started peeing.

That's when it happened. I suddenly noticed, too late to stop – Audrey across the street was seeing me peeing! A spotlight on me! Then noticing, after she stopped looking at me, she just went on. But part of <u>me</u>, never has.

Dad, that's what happened.

"That's it? That's what you're so upset about?!"

"Yes, dad, that's it."

"That's ridiculous!"

"Sorry Dad, but that is how it feels."

"Ridiculous! But ok, let's see what the jury thinks."

"Ok."

"What do you think?"

6. Being thirteen and titillation

We were all about 12: Eddie, me, my sister and Lorraine, sitting on the floor of my living room, talking. It began I think when we started talking about Houdini: *He could get out of anything!* So maybe it was Eddie who suggested: "Let's tie someone up and see if they could get out of it."

I liked the idea: I thought I could get out of anything! Maybe Eddie thought so too, that's why he thought of this game? Or maybe he had even a better reason?

I wanted Lorraine to go first: "Lorraine, want to go first?" "We tie YOU up?"

Lorraine maybe became a corporate executive when she got to be 37? or a dentist? But, for now, she was only 13 and was already stacked. She seemed shy, but wanted to do this; the combination felt thrilling.

Believe me, before we even started to get some rope, I was already thinking: "Exciting, yes tie her up!"

She lied down, or was it laid down, ready, easily. She was not hating this.

I tied her feet, Eddie and my sister: her hands behind her back. She was Eddie's sister, but he seemed fine about that. After all, my sister was probably next.

Then, the <u>ethical</u> plan was: We would set the time clock. If you could not get out of it in 5 minutes….. we could remove…? take your shoes off? There was no objections to that.

She was all tied up; we said "Go!" Lorraine struggled. It certainly did seem like she struggled. We watched. I got worried: one of the knots

13

seemed to be loosening. But, no fear, by then she only had about 30 seconds left.

Then the clock bell went off. What a wonderful sound. I was too scared to remove anything on her, but Eddie removed her shoes, my wonderful friend Eddie [great to have a wonderful friend] Eddie started it; took her shoes off. That was it, great, now, I thought, we all thought: here comes a whole avalanche!

So, I just loosened the belt on her jeans. My sister opened the first button on her blouse. [What a wonderful sister I had.]

Meanwhile, off, let's say, in Nevada the sun was setting, the moon started to rise, the stars came out.... But soon, wonderfully, Lorraine was still tied up....and almost nude!

Then, it happened!

We heard the elevator stop outside my Apt. door. It was my parents! They were talking in the hall as they slowly got out their keys to open the door. "Quick", I yelled: "Pick her up, pick her up!" We had to carry Lorraine into the bathroom! My sister went with her.

My parents immediately came into the living room: "Hi, guys been here long? Is there someone in the bathroom?" Eddie and I smiled: "Oh, Lorraine is in there... with Trisha."

"Oh."

We kept smiling. It felt like two weeks smiling at my parents, with my parents looking at us kind of microscopically, for two weeks.... before Lorraine and my sister finally came out of the bathroom. We kept smiling.

The four of us had entered *puberty* ....that would be with us the rest of our lives.

7. I remember all the words to that song

What song? This song:

"Hi over head the skylarks sing, they never rest at home. But just like me they love to sing as all the world we roam. ValderRee, ValderRaa, ValderRee, ValderRaa haa haa haa haa… ValderRee, ValderRaa, my nap sack on my back."

What is it about this song?

I was in the eighth grade at P.S. 82 in the Bronx. I was in Mrs. Morris's wonderful chorus class. Every month, besides just having our whole chorus perform, Mrs. Morris would pick a couple of kids to do a solo in front of the whole auditorium.

Finally, after stretching my hand out so hard my arm almost stretched out of my shoulder [I did this every week she asked for volunteers] she picked me. She picked three of us. We were going to sing the three verses of: "The Happy Wanderer". She played the music of the song for us several times so we could practice the melody. It was easy. The melody kept repeating. Then she gave us each our short little stanza [just two sentences] on a 3x5 card. Lloyd would sing the first stanza, then I would sing the next, then Jeffrey would sing the third.

"No problem" I thought, she thought, we all thought. The lunch bell rang. We were to memorize our little stanza over lunch time to sing in the auditorium, right after lunch. I memorized it easily: yes, just two sentences, each sentence rhyming. Here was my stanza. I remember it well:

"High over head the skylarks sing, they never rest at home. But, just like me they love to sing as all the world we roam." "Valderee, Valdera, Valderee…." No problem.

We all came back after lunch, and then heard the bell ring for the auditorium period. Mrs. Morris escorted the three of us and the whole chorus, down the back stairs to the back of the stage behind the curtain. Up front in the auditorium about 500 kids of my school were now slowly taking their seats. We were all excited and nervous behind the curtain… looking forward to our performing, being stars to 500 kids who would know us…forever.

Then the auditorium [we could hear it from behind the curtain] slowly got very quiet. Mrs. Morris left us from back stage and went out to the piano in front of the stage. And then, with a chord, signaled Lloyd, me and Jeffrey to come out and stand side by side at attention on the stage, facing all the kids, all the teachers, parents, and the principal… all looking at us. It felt thrilling, like I was on the top of a mountain.

Mrs. Morris smiled at us and then played the song's melody, as an Introduction, and then stopped. Then she played Lloyd's chord.

Lloyd stood more at attention and then sang: "I love to go a wandering along the mountain track, and as I go I love to sing, my nap sack on my back." Then all of us sang: "Valderee, Valeraa, Valeree, ….."

I stood there knowing: here it comes: me, I'm next. Lloyd's part was almost over. I could feel a: "now you go" coming right toward me. They were still singing: Valdereee…, but soon, here it comes, I very soon go.

The refrain: Valderees…. ended. The music stopped. I looked at Mrs. Morris, she looked at me, she winked at me, she looked down at the piano, and played my chord.

I heard it, I remember hearing it. I inhaled. She waited a second, then another second. Then, she played the chord again. I heard it, I really heard it, but:

I could not remember any of the words, none of them! Not a single word.

I know these words very well now, 61 years later, but then, when she played the chord…. Nothing. Mrs. Morris stopped smiling, looked very hard at me and played the chord again, this time very loud. I tried very hard to remember them, very hard… then:

I fainted and fell off the stage.

I think the entire auditorium started screaming and laughing. I don't know, because I had totally blacked out.

I woke up in the Gym. I was glad to be in the Gym, rather than on that stage not knowing any of the song. They had me keep my head between my legs for a long time, till I could finally regain full consciousness and leave the Gym.

However, for the next two years, whether I was in the school's hallway or on the staircase or in the school yard… at least 5 kids a day would point at me and say: "There's that kid that fainted and fell off the stage."

Sixty one years later, I remember every word of the song, especially my part; I can sing it for you now:

"Hi over head the sky larks sing, they never rest at home, but just like me they love to sing as all the world we roam." But, not then.

8. The great lesson when Eddie
went to the bathroom

When you grow up on a block, there is a chart somewhere that keeps track of who is best on the block at stick ball, hide-and-go-seek, telling jokes and running. You are on that block ranked. Every game you play, every joke you tell, and every race you enter... you know it will affect your ranking on your block. And of course you try to be included in games, and be with kids, who have high rankings; otherwise, you are a loser.

The same goes for, or even more especially for, playing Monopoly! This is one of the most serious engagement events you can do during your whole entire life during your whole childhood. Winning or losing at Monopoly when you are a kid feels like it decides whether you will ultimately be successful at life, and of course: real estate, business ownership, car ownership, girl ownership, going to college; almost as important as trying to get on TV, or be a rock n'roll star. Especially, that you did this "game" [it was not just a game!] in front of and with the kids on your block, and in one of their houses. All your friends were there, so this was the World.

No one wanted to be the banker in Monopoly; a busy job, and you could make a math mistake in adding up the fake money [it was real!] in front of your friends. However, to feel important, I would often volunteer to be Banker. Eddie was often the giver-outer of hotels, and deeds.

One day Eddie and I decided to play just Eddie and me. We had been playing with others our whole entire lives, since we were 8 years old. [We were now 12.]

Here's the thing, and the most important thing about that day and this game: **I had never, ever beaten Eddie at Monopoly!** In a way, even while I watched TV, even while I did my homework from 3rd grade till 7th grade, while I ate, while I slept… in the back of my mind, all those years, secretly they all knew, I knew: **I had never, ever beaten Eddie at Monopoly!** So that day, I think it was mid-April, we decided to play Monopoly in Eddie's Apt., just Eddie and me.

Yup, I decided to be Banker, Eddie the deeds and the hotels. [That day, during this important game: it was as if we were in an entire Stadium, with bleachers, and even guys selling hot dogs…in Eddie's Apt.] I gave out the money: 2 five hundreds, 5 one hundreds, 5 tens….etc. I chose the car, Eddie chose the cannon. I, of course, felt nervous. I rolled the dice, got 2 fives, a 10; he got a 2 and a 3, only a five. Thus I got to go first.

Somewhere it started to snow in a forest, the clouds covered the moon, it started to rain somewhere; meanwhile… soon Eddie owned Park Place and Boardwalk, had a hotel on each, had one Get Out Of Jail Free Card, already owned three of the four railroads, had at least $500 more than me…and I was losing. I was getting depressed and scared, scared the next day on my block all of them knowing what had happened and…. my lower ranking.

Eddie, however, looked agitated. What was wrong? Finally, he admitted it; he had to go to the bathroom. He got up, and quickly left the room for the bathroom just past the kitchen.

I was alone. No one was in the living room. My parents were at work, all the kids on the block were in their houses, the whole Bronx was busy - not able to see me. I looked over at all the money sitting in the Monopoly box: millions! I should've taken about a month to decide what to do, but I did not. From inside, me my hand reached out and I took 2 five hundreds. Once in hand, I had to hide it into my money. Now, no turning back. Done. I think I felt great…for about 2 seconds. Then, here comes Eddie.

I tried to kid around as usual, but had trouble being as funny as I was before. I don't think he noticed I was nervous. He just kept shooting the dice when it was his turn, and I when it was my turn.

In the next half hour, it felt as if two weeks went by. Since I kept having so much money, even when I landed on him, Eddie was starting to lose. I could buy more properties than he could, he landed on me more, I bought more properties, he landed on me more. The entire earth was shifting. Finally, at 5:16pm….Eddie was out of money. Eddie lost!

You would think that the birds would all fly into the sky, that crowds would cheer on mountains, that the whole block would celebrate…. But none of this happened. Eddie had to get ready, his mom would be home soon. I, of course, had to go home too. So, as if to do the same "goodbye", I did; but it was not the same. I left. I left, but walking down the hall to my apt., going in, then going to sleep that night, then waking up, going to school, going into 9th grade, then 10th, then eventually to college… I have never been the same. There was no celebration on my block and…. though I waited, there was no celebration inside me. Every store I passed, every train I was on, every job interview I had, every girl friend I had, every place I went….knew I had cheated. I got dam nothing from taking those 2 five hundreds! Well actually…I did: A lesson.

9. Missing Leona

If you were able to go back to the Bronx in 1954, and go up to the top floor, to a hidden flight of stairs, of building: 1726 Davidson Ave., you would see a 13 year old boy working passionately there very hard. Working on what? Trying to cut a silver dollar in half with a hack saw, holding it difficultly with his hands, and then trying to put a hole in it with a nail for a chain so it can be a necklace. A secret project. Why is he doing this?

Leona.

[She was also 13.] He has heard she is leaving the Bronx with her family next week to go to ….a place he has never heard of. He thinks that he will never see her again. He is trying to cut this silver dollar in half so he can give her one half that hopefully she will put around her neck for the rest of her life. He will wear the other half on his neck for the rest of his life.

Leona: adorable, blonde, angelic; she even had dimples. Her smile, even if not at Howard, lit up everything within blocks. Even the movements of her arms and hands were kissable. Her voice, her blue eyes, her short blonde hair - all glowed. I wanted to lick her like an ice cream cone. If I had had the courage, and no one was watching, I would've hugged her deeply, right on the street. But then I would not have been able to stop my whole body from cuddling and wrapping around her, crazed.

But, I was only 13, scared of girls, and thus, did not do that: I was terrified to even be near her.

She, with great risk and courage, was my first date, the first date I tried in my whole life. It was so frightening that I don't even remember how I asked her. It was to the movies. I barely remember walking to these movies. She was so near me when we walked that I walked kind of in a coma. Then, I was terrified that I would drop some of the coins from my pocket to pay the woman in the ticket booth. I am sure that Leona was probably watching me do all this, so I dared not look at her. We went in.

I have no idea what movie we saw. I was so scared sitting right next to Leona that I had to use all my concentration to not accidently cough, or breathe wrong, or, *god forbid*: accidently touch her.

There was a movie up there, I do remember images flashing on the screen, but mainly the problem was: Oh my god! Leona was sitting right next to me alone [though there were over 200 people in the theater].

This movie, to me, lasted 10 hours. About 9 of those hours was spent working very hard on my major goal: to slowly move my left arm near Leona, then place it on the top back of her seat, then slowly move it down…. to accomplish: *put- my- arm- around- Leona*: a major developmental task of my whole childhood.

After about a half hour, I was able, inch by inch, to get my arm up around to the top of her seat, but carefully, of course making sure I did not accidently touch her. [I certainly did not want her to catch me doing this.]

There, finally: I was able to get my arm on the top of her seat. I was on third base. However, to get to home plate felt like getting up the courage to jump across Niagara Falls. So, I had my arm up there on the edge of her back seat… for about an hour.

Then a major problem-crisis happened: because the edge of the back seat was pressing against my arm for so long…. I began to feel pins and needles in my arm; my arm was falling asleep. I suddenly couldn't move my arm.

[Leona, never stopped looking at the movie; she, I think, even laughed during the movie. At what? I have no idea. Remember: I never saw the movie.]

Finally, the movie ended, but I never got my dead arm from the top of her seat to around her to even touch her far shoulder. Probably good, I would have had a stroke, at 13 years old.

Leona did leave the Bronx. Yes, I did give her her half of the silver dollar. She just said: "Thank you", and continued to talk to her girl friends. I don't think she knew what it meant, or I meant, and I was too frightened to try to explain. She just walked away from to be with her girl friends.

I have never seen Leona ever again.

Parts of me are still missing Leona, and those days. I am, 62 years later, still attracted to any woman who is blonde.

I would like to go back and help that little 13 year old boy.

I would like to go back to him on the steps working there so hard, congratulate him for the man he will become, and help him on that first date, and show him all will be all right when he gets older. **I** would do the paying at the movie for him, sit next to him as he sat next to Leona, and help him, within two minutes, put his arm around Leona; even maybe help him place his hand caressingly on the back of her neck.

I would help him, now 62 years later, find Leona, maybe in…..Toledo? I would go up to her house with him, knock on her door, and when she opened it, wink at her…. And, then I'd give him the courage to give her a big, long kiss.

There are two Leonas: One who is now also 75 like me, has maybe two kids and four grandchildren and remembers nothing of this.

And then there's another Leona: who is now sitting on a sunny beach alone somewhere, looking off at the ocean. Her hair is still blonde, she is still very young, and she is pressing her hand against her heart, against the half silver dollar hanging from her neck, while she is sadly missing me.

10. Not just a dog

Some dogs are not just dogs. The ones we have, that also have us, are not just dogs. They are as much "us" as our brothers and sisters, as close as: across- the- table-being-with-a-loved-one. And, since we can do with them what would feel embarrassing with people [roll on the floor with them, tickle their bellies, play bite with them...] they are even closer.

Dogs do the hunger we have *to be listened to* – deeply and very well. They never interrupt; or if they do, it is to lick us to acknowledge that they understand us, feel us, and to tell us that they appreciate the attention we give them. Unlike our friends, they always look at us when we talk. We feel that they see us and know us. They also feel seen. Doing this with them is more concentrated than holding hands with a person. And we can talk to them for a long time. If they get fidgety, it is not because they are tired of listening; it is because their love of being attended to - gets so filled – they need to fidget from being loved so much, for such a long time.

We too get fidgety as we talk to them. We are not losing patience. It is that our love of this listening/loving together, goes into our hands – so we have to pet them; in this petting, we both get petted.

Luckily for me my family got a German Sheppard puppy when I was 15. Thus began my entrance into feeling close, protective and loving, a widening change in my whole life, due to my dog "Major".

This was my first real loving. I did not love Major because he was pretty, like Leona. Nor did I love him because I needed him like I needed my parents, or to get something. I loved Major because I could feel he was sometimes scared, sometimes sad, sometimes lonely, sometimes vulnerable, often needy of care and attachment to me and my family; he voiced what I needed and felt, but often did not notice in myself. And he was humble; he did not ask for too much, a bit afraid of being annoying, like me.

I wanted him happy. My happiness was his wagging his tail. Then, we were both happy. Often doing for him made me happier than doing for me. Yes, this was my first real loving.

And we did things together: He always faithfully ran for the ball I threw for him; and he got it for me. Yes, he got it for him too, but for-bringing-it-to-**me**, and I was for him too. And we did this for each other, giving warm playfulness, tickle-teasing and and just him/me kidding around, back and forth, back and forth. I often got worried he was getting tired. But, he seemed to say, "I'm all right. If you're all right, let's play more!" and he ran for the ball again.

Years later, we moved out of the city to the country. There, I walked Major almost every night. There were few houses there, and lots of dark woods all around on dark country roads. I had to bring a flash light to see the road, except when the moon was out. The darkness all around at night was scary; but not with Major. Major was a large German Sheppard, weighed over 110 lbs., on his hind legs stood 6'4"! He protected me like a German Sheppard in World War II. A lion could not attack me. I was safer in this darkness with him than walking down a street on a sunny afternoon. Here, at night, he was more master than I, smarter, more skillful, more aware. I was now following him. He did not need me as much as I needed him. He took over *watchfulness* for both of us. I was now in his care. He was a great animal; I was just a human.

One day I was sitting in a rocking chair on my porch reading. Major was lying down next to my chair, I thought sleeping. My buddy Ronnie came up behind me and teasingly began to put his hands over my eyes. Major knew Ronnie very well; played with him and me almost every day. As Ronnie's hands came behind me, suddenly Major leaped off the floor, jumped over me, and carefully grabbed Ronnie's hand in his mouth, and all in one giant move - pulled Ronnie to the floor. Ronnie was unhurt, but shocked and terrified. Major thought that Ronnie was going to hurt me.

Major and I both grew older, of course. When he was about 9 years old, Major started to feel pain in his back legs. We soon found out it was cancer. Eventually, after months of watching him in pain, and not being able to fix it, we knew we had to eventually take Major to be "put down". I rode in the car with my sister and Major to the Vet. But, when we arrived, I could not find the ability to get out of the car and take him in. My sister had the strength. She came out of the Vet without Major.

Of course, Major could not live forever. Nor could my friend Irwin, nor Danny. Ros has also died. My parents have both died. All of us listening to this - will die.

However, during all this living, there are some special hugs: not just at graduations, or birthdays, or weddings…. There are some special hugs just for some dogs. Some dogs are not just dogs.

I know: You want to hear more. You want me to tell you more about Major: us playing with a stick together, him sleeping next to me, me playing being-a-dog with him, or our running together…. I know, you want more? Well…, me too.

11. Who was my mother?

My mother, with the encouragement and assistance of my father, tried to abort me when she was pregnant by jumping off tables and running in her 9th month. When I was a toddler, she did not protect me when my father would take off his belt, whip me, yelling at me in full temper - such that even now at 74, I still sometimes have to fight the feeling that I am ugly and worthless. My mother did not stop him, barely saying, "Enough Al, enough."

My mother, in front of Arlene, who was also only 8, scolded me for leaving my socks on the floor, scolded me, embarrassed me in front of Arlene, as I had invited her from next door to watch TV with me. Arlene was a girl and I was scared of girls. It took a lot of courage for me to invite Arlene over. But, right there, in front of Arlene, my mother started yelling at me for leaving my socks on the floor. Arlene kept her head forward as if she was still watching TV, as I got smaller and smaller. Then my mother banished me to my bedroom; "You're going to sleep, right now!" I walked crying to the bedroom, past Arlene, feeling decapitated in front of Arlene.

However, my mother got even worse: I had taken my clothes off banished to the dungeon-like bedroom, then me only in my underwear, and my mother yells from the living room: "You get in here! You left another sock here on the floor!" I yelled back, crying, "Sorry, please stop yelling at me." ["In front of Arlene", I wanted to say.] My mother did not stop. Instead, she yelled back: "Get in here right now and pick this sock up!"

I could not: I was in my underwear; Arlene was still right out there. She would see me crying and see me in my underwear. I would rather have died. I did: My mother forced me out of the bedroom into the living room to pick up my sock. I died then, for years. My rage, and a kind of death-knife, went into me; and I wanted to kill my mother. But, I could not. I was only 4 feet tall and only 8 years old. And I still needed her.

My mother also lied a lot. For example: One time she was putting the dishes away in the kitchen closet and dropped my father's favorite glass and broke it. Later, when he came home, [I sat always nervous at the dinner table: scared of my father, worried my sister would get me in trouble, watching my phony smiling mother....] my father asked my mother: "Where is my glass, that glass I love?" My mother, smiled, looked straight at him, past me, and said: "What glass?" He continued: "You know that glass I always love...." Hidden slings and arrows went back and forth across the table. My mother persisted: "What glass? I have no idea what you mean." I went into shock. The shock? My mother had the same look on her face when she talked to <u>me</u> that way, that same lying, false smile, but now <u>I knew</u> she was lying. She had the same look at my father when she talked to me! When she always talked to me?! When was my mother truthful? When was she lying? Who was she in there, behind her face? An evil witch?... that I still needed? I only had one mother.

The whole ground I lived on shook.

However.....

I have been crawling through all this dark emotional tunnel for years in therapy.... I have gotten stronger. I too now have been a parent, and now understand much more.

I have come to realize and feel that: my mother had me, her first child, when she was only 19! <u>19</u>! I had a child when I was <u>46</u>! and with pretty good finances, family support, friends, a good job... and yet still found this parenting job – a very difficult, sometimes exhausting project. My mother was only <u>19</u> when she had me, barely an older girl who suddenly had to be a woman, a mother, with almost no emotional or economic support from her family, nor my father's family, and to top it all: she was also scared of my father. The struggling poor young girl.

I think I remember my mother holding out her beautiful ring to me as she tried to coax me to take my first walking steps toward her when I was about a year old. She smiled warmly toward me, and lovingly encouraging me to try to walk toward her [holding out her beautiful ring to give to me]. She was beautiful, and I wanted to get all the way, five feet away, to her.

I did. She gave me her ring, and then hugged and held me lovingly for a long time [a long time certainly for me].

I play piano. Playing piano for me [who was as a child: overweight, lonely and felt inferior] has given me admiration from my friends, teachers, and eventually girls I was afraid of. Playing piano, playing my feelings [sometimes alone in my apt.] was therapy for me. It still is. It has earned me money, attention, compliments, even helped me help my daughter become a professional singer and performer.

My mother taught me how to play piano, when I was 5 years old. My father told me: "She always wanted a son who could play piano." Her mother had taught her, now she taught me. This ability has lifted my whole life. What a gift! And, when I sit down to play, my mother is with me. I have my caring mother.

My mother was really a young girl. Unfortunately: she was very pretty, sexy, with had big breasts [though my father says that they were empty; so she could not breast feed]. I am sure her attractiveness was part of the reason she had to get married. She got pregnant with my father probably pretty quickly. I am sure that my father was not only physically attracted to my mother, but that sex for both of them was a tranquilizer, an emotion to get away from their own burdens, aloneness, and their own needy and distraught childhoods. [My mother's father was often a harsh cold man; my father got too little of his mother.] My mother and father took refuge in each other, especially I am sure, holding each other at night, clinging naked to each other, to ward off all kinds of fears.

When my mother living in Florida reached 79, she was diagnosed with pancreatic cancer. [This cancer now my problem, but again, not her fault.] Every couple of weeks I would fly from NYC to see her as she got weaker. Toward her final days, she did something that was gallant: I asked her: "The next time I come to Florida, should I bring Jaimelyn?" [My daughter, her new granddaughter, who she seldom saw.] (Who, at 9 months old, took her first walking steps with my mother, just as I had done 45 years before.)

My mother listened carefully to my offer to bring her and I am sure she desperately wanted to see her for the last time. But, upon asking her, she just sat there for about 30 seconds silent, just thinking and feeling.

Then she said to me, directly into my eyes less than a foot away: "No, she will get scared when she sees me like this; I don't want to do that to her."

Amazing: My once weak and troubled 19 year old girl-mother, who spent most of her adult life finding the strength to handle my fearsome father, nurture him midst her own burdens, while having to raise two initially unwanted children... now in terminal physical pain - musters the strength to love Jaimelyn – to give up forever her own want and need to have the last chance to ever see her little granddaughter.

In the last days down in Florida, I was able to get time with my barely alive mother alone, away from my father for a few minutes, who went into the kitchen to prepare some food. I knew I had only a short window of time alone with my mother. I kneeled down on the floor in front of my mother sitting in a chair, who was almost too weak to talk. I wanted to give her this. So I said to her, up close to her ear: "Mom, are you worried about anything?" She thought, but quickly answered with a tilt of her head toward the kitchen: "Him."

I said, "I'll try to take care of him". She nodded her head in thank you.

Then, I looked at her long; she looked directly at me during this long time. I said, "Anything else?" She kept looking at me, almost into me; I could feel she was trying to mount her courage. So instead, I did it: "Mom, are you worried I think you were not a good mother?" She looked at me even more piercingly [she had known me all my life] and said: "Yes, I am worried about that."

[Mark Twain reports: "When I was a boy of 14, my father was so ignorant I could hardly stand to have the old man around. But when I got to be 21, I was astonished at how much the old man had learned in seven years."]

My answer to my mother's worry? I had started to realize she was once as a young girl trying to be a mother; and I started to forgive her, but only a forgiveness of about 80%. I had started to realize all she had given me, in spite of her difficulties. Then, at her chair, I was only then only 55 years old. But, I assumed that, if I continued to grow, I would eventually forgive her 100%. But, by then, she would be gone.

So, I smiled, gave her a loving look, grabbed her hand and said assertively, 100%: "You were a good mother!" She smiled. I smiled back, looking at her for a long time.

I still am.

12. My mother inside me

My mother was once a little girl. As she got older she probably loved and needed her brother. But at 35, while eating at the family dinner table, he had a heart attack and died. My mother lost her only sibling.

My mother's father was almost deaf. So he would not just talk, but blare at everybody, of course at her too. Every comment he made, when he was not just depressed, was almost a yell. My mother's mother seemed to be mostly resilient, not mostly nurturant; a perseverer. She re-married, and married, and married…outliving three dying husbands: earthquakes and river rapids my mother was on the boat of. I am sure my mother had to do many tasks for her parents, managing all while maybe never getting a warm hug or embrace, needing to stay strong.

My mother also had the assets, but the emotional burden of, large breasts, being sexy, very pretty, and looking very caring and warm. She must have had to swat men away like flies, while yet needing their attention, a contradictory problem of guarding herself while needing their care, needy from having grown up in an often grating, emotionally *empty-of-affection* home.

Luckily, she met my father when she was 18. She must have sensed in him that he was lost too; and thus empathetically took care of him - as she needed, and perhaps to also have her lost brother again. She must've felt my father was riding rapids too, and so they got into the same boat together. She probably welcomed not only his fatherly protection but the *getting-away-from-it-all* sexual pleasure they could give each other. Then, at least she was held/wanted, and could hold and be held, <u>una</u>lone coming from her/their cold childhood. My mother slowly grew [she had to] the ability to handle whatever came her/their way, [did the resilience of <u>her</u> mother] to keep both she and my dad going, on top of the water.

However, the poor girl got pregnant at only 19, and with little help from her cold mother and deaf father, nor from my father's parents. Ashamed, she had to get married, already three months pregnant and then make the only home they/she could make. They [her the stronger engine] tenaciously pushed ahead, and loved each other, for each other, each taking care of the other's lost-child. Head toward the wind, never giving up, my mother pushed thru these difficult circumstances to be as *steel through butter.*

Later in their lives my parents owned a retirement residence in Florida that had on its property eight palm trees. "Eight Palms" was the name they gave to a small motel they bought that would be a business for them: a retirement residence for seniors.

However, they could not get a regular license to take care of non-ambulatory seniors, as this required red tape they could not qualify for. So, they did this Motel Retirement Residence for "healthy" retired seniors. My father entertained the residents with jokes, played checkers with them, and sang for them [supported by my mother at the piano]. He would also drive them to go shopping or to a movie. My mother cooked and cleaned. All was ok; they did well, together.

However, every once in a while a resident would break a hip, or their knees would give out and they would suddenly have trouble walking. Very sad. However, even more upsetting, since my parents did not have a license to house non-ambulatory seniors, these seniors had to leave, or the Board of Health would close down Eight Palms.

This disability would happen to my parents' residents about once a month. For example: One afternoon my father comes to my mother with tears in his eyes: "Rozy, Arthur, when I was playing checkers with him [my father played checkers with Arthur for over 3 years, every day, probably also trying to make him laugh]….tells my mother, teary eyed, "Rozy, Arthur got up from the table and fell; I think he broke his hip!" My father starts to cry. My mother understood immediately. She touches my father on the shoulder, but does not show a cry or even look sad. She becomes steel: "Al, I'll do it." She stops drying the dishes, walks straight to Arthur's room, and says to Arthur in bed, "Arthur, you have to leave!" Then walks back to the kitchen and says, calming my father: "It's done, I did it." She could do what was needed right on the spot and not let any emotions weaken what she had to do. A *resilient powerhouse*, earned back throughout her being a little girl.

While I was teaching high school in the Bronx, after preparing lessons, teaching all day till 3:30pm, I would get on the train to Manhattan. While riding the train from the Bronx to Manhattan, and back again in the morning…I marked papers, prepared lessons, memorized photos of the faces of my students… and also went to the New School for late night classes to get my Ph.D. …..for 13 years. I also got married while teaching college, while doing consulting work in schools, giving speeches, writing my first education book, publishing professional articles [or perish] and also trying to be a good new father to my new daughter. Those years were like inhaling, holding my breath, and gritting my teeth; also needing to go to therapy to handle all this, and my past. I wrote in the Preface to my Ph.D. dissertation: "I want to thank my mother for her resilience."

When I was 16 years old, I had to swim across a pool carrying a 25 lb. weight, then learning how to rescue a 200 lb. man faking drowning, study a book on Being a Life Guard, then take a written and performance test…. to become a Certified Life Guard. I did. By August of 1959 I was 17 years old, sitting up on a Life Guard Chair, a Life Guard for Mohegan Lake N.Y. I had to sit up there and never take my eyes off the water, off all those kids playing, splashing, horsing around, faking-fighting…., and keep deciding who was really in trouble or just playing. I had to not just always watch the water, but decide and decide hundreds of times: was I watching fun or fear. If I did not keep watching and watching carefully, one of those kids could DROWN; then I would have trouble sleeping the rest of my life.

One day, near the end of August, someone wanted to talk to me while I was up on the Life Guard Chair. I was trained, while on the Chair, to talk to people without looking at them; I needed to always keep my eyes on the water. Suddenly, from the corner of my left eye, I see a little girl [maybe 3 years old] wandering alone on the docks by the boats at the side of the lake. Suddenly she falls off the dock and into the water fully clothed with her shoes on. No one saw her except me. I knew she would quickly drown.

I do not remember jumping off the ten foot high Life Guard Chair, nor do I remember running as fast as I could, about 75 yards across the sand, dodging people on the beach. All I knew was:

I saw her fall and I was at the dock with her in my arms.

No one even knew why I was running; no one had seen her fall in. I did. Her parents were somewhere on a beach blanket casually talking to their neighbors.

I held her with her head down, hit her on her back a couple of times; she immediately threw up water, and started breathing again, and then cried. She was fine. It was over. It was over, she was ok. I gave her to her parents [who had run to me] and then I slowly started walking back to the Life Guard Chair but… I suddenly fainted and fell to the ground.

However, in about 10 seconds I was able to get up, and was strong again, and returned to the Life Guard Chair. I was OK. I could feel it, I knew it: I had been my mother.

13. Teaching

It's amazing that you can look at a ball in your hand and then throw it to someone out there who then receives <u>the same ball</u>. They now have the same ball that was in a totally different place, now with different people. This is amazing and wonderful. Why?

Because we are each locked up in our own world. I only have my eyes, my ears, only my taste and touch in my-world. But I can give you my ball, or give you all I see, tell you my world, and you can also give me <u>your</u> world! Our walls can be porous; we can touch and be with each other through these givings and tellings.

Teaching is the art-skill that does this powerful intimate break-through. Teaching is profound. If it were not for these teaching's-transfers, one to the next, to the next... over billions of years - we would not have evolved from one celled animals to be us. None of us would be here!

I often felt alone when I was a little boy. I felt isolated inside myself; I could not touch much outside me. People were on the other side of a glass wall. I was in solitary confinement, even as I sat at the dinner table, or walked through my living room, and especially as I lay in bed at night alone, only with me.

Then, one day when I was very young, I like hit a bell or rolled a ball toward my sister. Suddenly my sister had a reaction to me and from me. She jumped at the sound of my bell, or she got the same ball that I had rolled to her. She heard my sound and got what I had. That was wonderful. A "door" had opened: I had figured out: How: *to not be alone and felt a with, with another.*

I then wanted to do these with-exchanges a lot. But, I noticed that I had to aim my exchanges well to be able to get back a meaningful reaction. My seeing, feeling, showing had to be clearly accurate, or the walls would not become porous. So, I worked at it: *Teaching*. I noticed that I could actually make someone smile, and at me. I finally had some light coming in. I could then smile back and they did the same. Perhaps, they were alone in there too?

I especially began to tell them what felt strange to me [strange things made me feel lonely and scared]; and noticed that they felt better also. My teaching took the "strangeness" out of things for them and for me. I began to feel connections with other people. My aloneness began to dissipate. In my telling they got me, and I got them.

I was pulling myself out of a lonely dungeon. I had felt lonely on the street when I was 7, not good at playing ball, overweight, and always worried no one really would like me. All my conversations on my block were me not-being-real, but "trying to be liked". I had real conversations only with myself in bed at night about: my worries, loneliness, my scared feelings.

Except….when I told a joke. Then, I worded my feelings accurately, used them authentically, felt/watched my audience carefully to do the right timing… and put out my joke. And often: "I got them!" I was then in a glory spotlight; I had done: that *communication-power*: teaching.

I loved taking what felt confusing to them and making it un-confusing. To do this I had to also go be in their shoes, feel what I just said, and see if it was: "Now understood?" And, if I paid close attention, they taught me more how to teach them. I started to do what Mrs. Morris did, my great choral teacher in 8th grade: I gave content to them but placed it into my real, honest feelings. That was the powerful vehicle that drove their understanding / my teaching.

Teaching to me is about attachment to others. We attach, as we work together, as we each leave our own solitary confinement. You are glad to be out of your cell, and I am glad to be out of my cell, with you. And, wonderfully, this now bigger room is also more full of people; so much so that we forget there are walls.

We kind of wink when we have attached, when we have gotten each other. It is a subtle kiss, an intimate message. We get it *together*. You open your mouth, ears, feelings… and you let me in; we let each other in. When done, we walk away having held *more* than hands. And you take away what we held. Me too.

I wanted to be a teacher since I was 12. I went to college to be a teacher. I needed to be a teacher since I was **2**.

I will throw a ball to you. When you get it, it was my ball. So glad you get it, that WE get it. Teaching.

14. The prequel and becoming a father

I almost did not do the greatest most wonderful *life-project* that enhanced and gifted my whole life!

For years prior to this "project", I had been teaching in the Bronx full time high school, previously subbing, preparing lessons, marking papers, commuting on the subway, as I tried to eat a bagel and coffee.... Then teaching college, trying to publish [or perish] having to serve on committees, observed and evaluated twice a year, plus travelling for 13 years at night to Manhattan to finally [with the help of therapy] getting my Ph.D. ... when Karen, my wife of six years, suddenly tells me that she has decided that she wants to be a mother, coming through probably a tough decision herself, her biological clock ticking at 41 years old.

I thought: "What?! I am finally ready to have some freedom and money, we could run around the world together, be fun free spirits.... now, she wants us to have a child?! This was a wrench in my current desires. And she basically concluded: if I did not want to have a child, our relationship would begin to end.

What did I feel? Narrowly, most in the foreground of my feelings, I wanted my new growing freedom and subsiding stress, but did not want to lose my relationship with Karen. Being a father, at that moment [when I was not as emotionally as smart as I am now] meant to me: pressure again, more heavy responsibility, money worries again, and much more new "work".

I could not then feel or remember that: I loved kids all my life, loved entertaining them, that I loved being a great, fun, loving, caring camp counselor, camp director, then trainer of teachers since 1969 [subliminally trying to make better "parents" for vulnerable children]… caring for kids from the age of even before 16 till now in my early 40's - unconsciously actually giving them all the care I did not get when **I** was a kid: fixing little Howards, little vulnerable kids like I had been.

I not only had little care when I was a child, but got *bad* care: neglect, abuse, anger, put-downs, seldom attention, often very unwanted, irritation [to say the least] that I was even born [an accident] from needy parents, themselves needing better parents.

Did I then also worry that having a kid would be a "pain" in the ass like I was to my parents? I don't know. I was not good then at knowing my feelings: that often, unconsciously, I wanted to give to the little Howards who got so little.

This was certainly inside me: **this joy-power of healing kids**. But, "having a kid" right then, in my squinted vision, I immediately felt this "having a kid" was too anxiety provoking, and a loss of finally a-freedom-oasis I forefront wanted.

Also, what was even more burying of this *joy-power of enjoying healing kids* was: that when my sister was born, I was two. I then had the pain of being pushed aside. I got little before she was born, but much less when she came; she was my rival for my parent's attention, the little that they could give. For my parents, when my sister came, my parents had to take care of two "accidents"! They never wanted me in the first place, and now two!

And now: Karen wants a kid?! This was a visiting a haunted house without even much awareness I was in it.

"Uh oh!" In the back of my mind: "Here comes my sister again" to banish me, to take away again any "mothering-care" I got from Karen. These negative reactions to having a kid was the subliminal dread of: *here comes my sister again!* But, I did not fully realize this "threat", which tangled and blocked any feelings I had of healing and thus loving kids. I could not picture what the future would really be in this emotional tangle and stress.

[We do not realize that often it is not the future that is scaring us; it is actually the past that we fear, that it may come back again!]

Under upset, pressure and crossed fingers, and maybe sensing way inside that I loved kids, I put myself into therapy to sort this all out.

First, Dr. Mildred Schwartz, then Dr. James Sachs, and also exploring this "fear-not wanting a kid" in a peer-run therapy group. Early in these therapy explorations, I think I did start to sense the "intimacy" that would come into my life with this child/project, while also uncovering that my resistance to having a child was mainly the fear of having my sister being reborn again, and all that that did to me when I was little.

So, with "crossed fingers" that maybe this would be good and right for me, I started to work at getting Karen pregnant.

Why? I don't fully and clearly remember all the feelings that went into this decision, since I decided this over 30 years ago. Surely, Karen's probable leaving our relationship - if we did not have a child - was the initial push to try this "project". [I thank her now, greatly, for this initial push.] I was also putting myself into various therapy sessions, and that peer group of therapists. I also probably started to feel/realized I loved making kids happy, and was good at it. I also certainly began to realize that it was fear of *the coming of my sister* that was in large part the "resistance/fear" of having a child. I also, probably could feel that "intimacy" was so treasured in my life experiences; it is, 32 years later, perhaps the highest value in my life: closeness. But, then, all was in a fog; I was still growing, learning my feelings.

I must have really been committed to this project since we were able to get Karen pregnant <u>before</u> we made our successful, wonderful, Jaimelyn. Karen had a miscarriage of her first pregnancy in about the 3rd month. We were to call this baby: Nicky. I remember that we were walking across a bridge on our vacation in January of, I think, 1986, when I/we learned of this miscarriage. I do remember **not** <u>being relieved</u>; I think I was sad, already attaching to "Nicky". Obviously, we, [including ME], worked at trying again, I was *in* this project, since wonderful Jaimelyn did get conceived. J. I think she was conceived one of our nights in Sept. I remember working hard at it then. [Yes, since Jaimelyn was born 9 months later on May 28].

So, obviously I was **there** for this "project". However, notice above I say:

I almost did not do the greatest most wonderful project that enhanced and gifted my whole life!

Again, I certainly thank Karen for initially pushing me to do this.

Then, once Karen was pregnant again, my love, bonding and devotion grew and grew with this child. I kept myself in therapy, this time with Dr. Jim Sachs. I think Jaimelyn was in utero only 6 months when, with Dr. Sachs – a greater catalyst happened!

[We knew the sex of the child]. Dr. Sachs says to me in a session:

"What if this child being born is another little Howard [not your sister] but Howard as a girl?!"

Wow, did that cut through the fears I still may have had. I could then give what I did not get to a little Howard, an even more fragile Howard [as girls I felt were even more fragile]. I could protect and care for a new, second chance, fragile little Howard! What was left of the muddy dark fog of tangled emotions began to lift.

So that by the time that Karen was only pregnant about 5 months, I already began devoting myself to my new child. The more I devoted myself to this new myChild the more she was <u>not</u> my sister.

Karen, who knew my fears, so graciously let <u>me</u> name her: I honored Karen's father: James, and I loved and so respected my aging friend Lynda Wismer. With a little *French* input, I made her: "I love Lyn": *Jaimelyn!* **I** named her. She was mine, certainly not my displacing sister!

Thus, from initially "not wanting a kid", I began loving little **Jaimelyn** way before she was even born!

I went to baby classes when Jaimelyn was in utero, about 6 months before she was born: "CPR for infants"; "How to Bathe the Baby". I read about the stages in the pregnancy, went to every Dr. visit with Karen, started planning our home for Jaimelyn, e.g., her room. I went to birthing classes with Karen. I also remember a show with music in it and feeling Jaimelyn bouncing inside Karen to the music…… Jaimelyn became a major care-project for me even before she was born.

Then, I was very lucky: At the delivery, Karen got eclampsia, very high blood pressure. As a result, when Jaimelyn came out, they gave her to <u>me</u>, in order for them to work on Karen who was barely conscious and was in danger of having a stroke. I was to go off and feed little Jaimelyn a water bottle while they took care of Karen. I did, all alone with little Jaimelyn on the 30ᵗʰ floor of Mt. Sinai Hospital, looking out across Central Park.

This alone time with Jaimelyn was one of the most intimate, wonderful, life affirming times of my life. I talked to her, showed her Central Park out the window, and talked to her about coming into amazing: *being-alive.* I had her to myself, wonderfully. We were alone with each other. She was mine to care for and hold and make safe, and introduce her to the world and to being alive. Looking at her, talking to her was grander than looking at the whole ocean and all the stars. She, I think, heard me; we were Jaimelyn and daddy, and Miskeepoo, and Sima, and Dadem and JJ more and more with each other, all the way, more and more... all the way till today, 30 years later.

The rest of the story was/is all the same: devotion, giving her the attention I never got as a child, making her strong, teaching her about feelings, letting her have the joy of freely performing what was inside her, helping her do her imagination and feelings, being her attentive audience, giving her laughter, drama-thrills, teaching her about *time, being* her tutor for school... and slowly giving her that *secret* we must eventually tell: that we all have to end.... And to be strong and wide and thick for all of this - by wrapping it all up in closeness.

I [and Karen] made her feel **special**. I wrote to her in my journal: "Welcome to the world!"

And many poems for and about her:

I [we] have been allowed to create a little princess.
We've never done it before, but it seems that we've done a perfect job.

And she shall spin and shine like a crystal dancer.

*We blew life into a space that had not been
and now there shall be a dancer.*

*I will lift her, her arms raising high
and she will go from not realizing she is a child
to realizing she was a child.*

And I will know all of this long before she can even understand.

*And by the time I can explain it to her
and she realizes....I shall be old
watching her realize
I made her feel like a little princess.*

There's the stars at the beach at night. There's the expanse of the Grand Canyon at sunset.

There's the earth seen from the surface of the moon. And then, there's sitting on a small mountain of rock in Central Park watching my daughter play on a slide....

Each time I lift her out of her crib: there's that "stay up there!" feeling as when you do your first throw of your model airplane that you carefully glued and painted and held.

That "go!" you say as you let it go from your hand as you bend forward, hands on your knees:

"stay up there, go, go, stay up there."

Jaimelyn became the more-wide, more colorful glasses I saw my whole life through. I re-experienced the thrills of: seeing my first squirrel,

Halloween, blowing out candles…. Everything! The whole world became wider and deeper.

I dedicated my poetry book:

To my daughter: Jaimelyn, to whom I gave life, and by having her to love - gives it <u>more</u> back to me.

My father gave me little, but probably a better childhood than he had.

I gave Jaimelyn a much better childhood than I had.

However, there is one main thing missing from this description of what happened: Jaimelyn, rapidly became day by day [even as we looked out the window at Central Park] a real *person,* more and more, every second, minute, years….she grew. She, with everyday, became not a clinical project, nor a therapeutic healing of me, but more and more, a little, then bigger and bigger: a whole, full real person, more and more separate from me though I kept giving her more and more ME, putting more *who- I-am,* especially *m- grown-wiser Me,* into who she was becoming - as I continue to do to this very day.

We loved each other, more and more, not as a project, but as two separate fuller and fuller persons, both alive, both vulnerable, and within time's mortality, as we both learned, and keep learning from each other. Jaimelyn, this now great separate person, also now helps me grow!

As I wrote *and now add:*

Each time as I watch her:

like blowing a bubble from my own breath

that then floats on its own air to freedom

that then looks back at me, *we becoming ours, not just mine, then her's, then her own self*

looking at me, *able to give to me too;*

looking at her.

Our fingers are going into each other.

Even more wonderful that we now have separate hands loving, appreciating each other. Even greater that she is <u>not</u> mine; though so glad I chose to start her.

I almost did not do the greatest most wonderful life-project that enhanced and gifted my whole life!

15. My father inside me

My father was once a little boy.

I can see from photos that he worked at trying to be a gymnast, even tried to do boxing. He had five brothers, and two sisters; he born in the middle. However, one of his sisters [while his mother yelled out the window to guide her crossing the street at 7 years old] died, hit by a car right in front of his mother yelling from the window to warn her. My father probably loved this little sister. Now, he had only one sister, only one other warm female to make up for his stressed mother, the rest of his life. How did he deal with these feelings? Probably feelings he could barely bear to feel.

His mother [whose father was a baker, who held meetings in his bakery to help Jews in their Polish neighborhood, was murdered by anti-Semites] was only 17 when she took a month- long boat to the U.S. across the Atlantic Ocean to find her husband who had fled conscription into the army. However, her emotional weight on this boat was two-fold; she also carried with her, at 17 years old, her first child, her first son, my father's oldest brother. She went on to raise 7 others, learn English, carry coal up five flights of stairs, cook for all, tolerate her irresponsible husband, learn English...on and on.

My father got little from such a stressed mother. I am sure he was often lost among these turmoils. But, there was even worse for him:

He had some talent at being able to draw [I know this because he, with pride in this skill, taught me how to draw; showing me not only how to draw, but also showing me that he had this skill].

51

Why "worse"? because his younger brother was much, much better at this than my father. Eddie went on to be a famous cartoonist, established his own artistic studio, drew characters for TV commercials… and totally eclipsed my father.

No wonder at 21 my father must have been comforted and thrilled to find this beautiful, 19 year old girl: Rosalind being attracted and warm to him: my mother.

My father also wrote poetry, played the saxophone, the harmonica, sang, and wrote several songs: music and lyrics.

Worse: However, after he sent his best song to Paul Whiteman [a famous orchestra/radio show leader] he found out weeks later that his song was playing on the radio. However, every eighth note of his song was slightly changed with new words. His song had been stolen; the slight changes skirted the current copy right law and then went on to sell millions… but nothing for my father. My father was at first thrilled to hear his song on the radio while driving, but as he listened, and realized…he was devastated, depressed, almost the rest of his life, worse.

My father also cried easily. He easily felt sad, then comforted by my mother. Or he easily got angry and lost his temper. About once a year or so he would sit down at the dinner table and then slowly tell my mother that he had been fired again at his job. Why? He would explain: "Because this boss is a schmuck!" My father in the 20 years I can remember growing up living with him: had about 10 bosses all who turned out to be schmucks. My father could not take feedback. All feedback to him felt like harsh criticism he could not hear. His insecurity could not tolerate not doing well. He would just rage or get depressed against his failings.

But, and this is a big "But", my father, lucky for me: always felt a lot, and expressed all these feelings…in poetry, song, sadness, drawings, trying to be liked by telling funny stories, or by telling my mom the feelings he was going thru. My father, fueled by his need to have caring attention, and to be good at something, hopefully to a whole audience, was a "ham". He was always either sad or out there: but almost always *emotional.*

My daughter is now a paid performer. She has thousands of fans in the U.S. and in Europe who come and applaud, even scream, ovations when she is onstage either singing some of her original songs, or acting out one of her fifteen or more comic characters. She gets millions of hits from fans on YouTube, raised over $14,000 in just 10 days for a CD she created of her music thru KickStarter, and has performed at MGM studios, and at Second City, Chicago.

I kidded with her role playing when she was two years old, where I interviewed her dolls; she spoke for each one as their mother. By the time she was five years old, I could walk into her room and just ask her, e.g., "How long have you had this restaurant?" And without a pause, she would answer: "Five years; I started when I built a small one in Manhattan, and now I have these restaurants also in China. We serve elephant ears, hot dogs, pop corn...."

Every time in school that there was a talent show, I played the piano for her and she would enter. She almost always won. The audience was astounded that this little girl could mesmerize. Jaimelyn, since being little, has never been shy. A "ham" from the start. [In Shakespeare's "As You Like It", starring Jaimelyn in her senior year at colleg, there were over 2,000 in the audience when she was only 21 years old.] The larger the audience - the more confident and powerful she became. The fixed attention from the audience was like her swallowing fountain-fuel to perform with even more impact. Then that impact she had, that she knew happened to the audience, gave her even more fuel. On and on.... a-chain-reaction-performing-powerhouse. She still does that, now, more and more.

My daughter *is my father* now singing and emotionally acting... successfully. With my feeling his sadness and failures...I kind of pumped him into her, past his depression at not succeeding. He lives, revived and finally successfully performing, in my dear great Jaimelyn. I could not resurrect or save my father.

But, I did build a monument to him: my emotionally smart, great performer: Jaimelyn. **I** couldn't be the performer he wanted to be. I had some of his ability, but did not have enough *trying-courage*, nor the full competence needed, nor did I have enough of an able-to-love supportive father. Jaimelyn does.

16. A major decision

One of the worse sufferings one can carry, like a knife you can't pull out, is self-loathing, hating yourself.

When our daughter was 2 years old, we had to make a major decision, that if decided wrongly – she would have to undergo a serious operation at 12 years old, then be debilitated for over a year, and feel an inferior sense of self - for the rest of her life. And, I would hate myself for the rest of my life if I influenced this decision with her mother and made the wrong decision for hurting our daughter.

What was this decision? What would you have decided?

When my daughter started to walk at 10 months old, we noticed that she walked with her feet not straight forward, but turned in, so that her right foot turned toward her left foot, her left foot turned toward her right foot; any more so, she might trip over her own feet.

I worried that, as she got older, this "turn in" of her feet would get worse? She would grow up crippled, never be able to walk well, or run, always be teased by her friends and never be able to be in any sports. She would always be self-conscious, feel ugly….and kind of hiding for the rest of her life.

With fear, and her too young for her to understand any of this. I took her to an orthopedist when she was 11 months old who specialized in these kinds of childhood disorders. He evaluated her for about 15 minutes and then recommended that she be forced to wear her right shoe onto her left foot and vice versa, and sleep with a bar: ***The Denis-Bro Bar,*** on her feet that pulled her feet outward every night for years. So, we tried these methods…for a couple of weeks.

However, we could see that these methods were hurting her all the time. It was hard to watch her always in discomfort, she feeling awkward almost all the time.

At the urging of friends and family, my wife and I went for a second opinion to another child orthopedist. This doctor immediately understood the methods that we were trying. However, before he gave us his opinion, he wanted to take an x-ray of Jaimelyn's hips and legs. Trusting he knew what he was doing, we consented. He said we could do this right now.

He ushered us into an x-ray room and asked that we have Jaimelyn put on a white gown. Then, he explained to me: "Mr. Seeman, I want you to hold your daughter down on this x-ray table, her hips against the table, her lying face up. It is important that you hold her down this way, so her hips do not move, or we will not get a clear x-ray. Do you understand?" I don't think Jaimelyn knew what was going to happen.

The Dr. had me put on a lead jacket to protect myself from the x-rays. Then first soothing little Jaimelyn, I put her first sitting, then lying down, on the table. Then, the Dr. instructed me, that when he says: "Go!" how to hold Jaimelyn down, yet still exposing her to the x-rays from her waist to her thighs. I was to do this for ten seconds. I got in position. Jaimelyn looked scared, bewildered: "What was going to happen?!" was the look on her face. Then, the Dr. yelled: "Go!" I leaned forward, Jaimelyn's face to my face….and held her down.

This was one of the most upsetting things I had ever done. Jaimelyn first looked at me scared: "What was daddy doing to me?!" "Let me go!" was her look. I tried talking to her calmly, but I must've seemed to be suddenly *a lying daddy*: talking calm yet forcefully holding her down against her will. The 10 seconds seemed to last for an hour. Jaimelyn kept looking at me, "Let me go, are you my daddy? Where is my caring daddy?"

Finally it was over. I let go. She was relieved, yet bewildered. I must have spent hours trying to explain why I had to do this to her to have her trust me again, to trust people, men, doctors…. Only weeks later, could she finally again place her head on my chest…. to relax and be held again. But, it took a long time… and for me, I am still not over it.

But, Jaimelyn's feet? Her legs?

The doctor called us in for an appointment about 3 days after the results of the x-ray. He sat us down, took a deep breath and sternly said to us: "What I am about to tell you will be very hard for you to do, but I really advise this and I think I am right." "What? What?" We asked: "I think regarding your daughter's feet and legs, you should do…NOTHING. From what I see, her hips are fine; I think that her legs will just, over time, straighten out, and she will just grow out of this naturally, I think."

"Are you sure?"

"I think I am correct. But, if I am wrong, when she is about 12 years old, she will need a major operation to correct her legs, and that will then take much rehabilitation; ….but I don't think I am wrong."

"You think we should just…..do NOTHING?"

"Yes."

"If you want, you can continue for months and months, maybe years, to put her through wearing shoes on the wrong feet and use the bar on her feet at night. But I think this is all unnecessary. She will naturally just grow out of this."

Dazed, scared, my wife and I said we would think about this, thanked the doctor and left his office. Of course, my wife and I discussed this over and over. We finally decided: For the next couple of years…. We would do: NOTHING. Of course, we always watched Jaimelyn walk….every day, every time she got up from a chair to walk.

One of the worse sufferings one can carry inside, like a knife you can't pull out, is self-loathing, hating yourself.

When Jaimelyn was 11 years old, the school district in lower Manhattan promoted a running race around a mile long track for 10 to 12 year olds. About 60 kids, feeling they were very fast, registered for the race; Jaimelyn registered.

It was a sunny day when we got to the track, Jaimelyn, all suited up, walked slowly out to the start line of the track where all the kids were gathering. My wife and I took a seat in the stands. We were to watch Jaimelyn try to run as fast as she could, remembering our painful decision when she was 2 years old.

After explaining the rules to all the kids, and lining them up, the stood readied in front of all the kids. The kids were ready. We were ready. Finally, the referee waved a flag and yelled: "Go!"

We watched her, and watched her, all the way from that x-ray table to now round a mile long track. Years of watching her walk went by. Now on this track, for about ten long minutes, Jaimelyn ran and ran, she ran as hard and as fast as she could. The expression on her face was: *determined!*

How'd she do? Of the 60 fastest kids in the whole school district of over 3,000 kids, of course, she did not win the race. She came in 2nd, about 2 feet behind the fastest kid in all of lower Manhattan! Jaimelyn's feet and legs? Perfect!

17. Jaimelyn leaving

Jaimelyn, sitting in the back seat of our car says, "No thanks, I'll be fine. Thank you. Talk to you soon. Love you." And, then opens the car door, gets out, blows us a kiss and we watch her walk across a lawn. Then, she turns once again towards us, waves, blows us another kiss, and then opens the door to a building and goes into her dormitory. Our Jaimelyn has just gone to college.

When I diapered her, I lifted her by holding both of her feet up in the air and kissed them, then continued putting on her new diaper, talking to her. She looked at me long during all this. We smiled. We did this a hundred? times. Then later, the similar with putting on her shoes, tickling her, then teaching her numbers, holding her in my arms, especially when she was sick, toweling her off at 2 years old from her bath while singing "Oklahoma" to her, reading children's books to her as she leaned against my shoulder, ….on and on.

Jaimelyn has just left to go to college; she now can do lots by herself. We will see her in about…one month. However, I saw her almost every second, from: on my shoulder, to watching her sleep, to her doing her homework, helping her sing by playing the piano for her, clean up her room, bring home with Elizabeth to her so they could do: "dress up".

Jaimelyn has just gone off by herself to …College? Nah, she's too little to go to college!

Every time I see her, I wrongly picture her age by years. I go meet her at the airport from her Apt. in Chicago, and she is 27, but expect that she looks like 12 years old. I quickly recover and do not tell her of my fading myth.

There are signs that tell me time is going by: the stores that closed on my street, my back is hurting more, my car does not work as well…..But seeing Jaimelyn is the real reminder of time, and me older and older. Time goes mostly through and with my Jaimelyn.

I remember playing piano for her so she could sing: "The Sound of Music" for her 5th grade talent show. She does well. A year later, I arrive early to get a good seat for her 6th grade's *end of year show*, and wait for my Jaimelyn to be up there on stage. Finally, she goes up and sings; she is now Maria, the star of the whole show! They applaud, she smiles and bows with great satisfaction. So do I. Then, years go by: I watched her do: "A Christmas Carole"; she is now Tiny Tim in an off-Broadway theater. Then, years later, in "As You Like It"; she becomes Shakespeare's: *Rosalind* [coincidently my mother's name!] at the University of Michigan. On and on.

Now, today, Jaimelyn opens the door to her dormitory, and walks in. Now I cannot see her anymore. But, I tell myself, I will see her… in 2 months. I will see her then in 3 months. I will see her. But, scared-knowing: I will not see my same Jaimelyn again. She will grow and change when I am not there.

That never happened when she was one or two, or even five. I made sure I would almost constantly see her grow. But, now… I cannot. She has gone into that dorm. She said, "No thank you" to: "Can we carry this last box for you?" But, no. She will carry this box in by herself. By herself.

Even my home now misses Jaimelyn. The little puppet Ernie, who talked to her thru my hand when she was 2, also misses her. My piano misses her. The TV. Her block. The bagel store. P.S. 41. Even the squirrels in Washington Square Park… miss little Jaimelyn.

Once a blossom burst in the Universe and little Jaimelyn was born, out of Karen, into my arms. I kept giving more and more life into her, and yes, it worked. She is all blossomed-grown up. I sometimes wish I had not done such a good job so fast.

However, in a way, I am too going into that college dormitory. I am under her. I taught her how to walk, even how to carry her boxes. What an amazing successful project [much grander than my model airplanes].

What an amazing successful full person she is, this MyJaimelyn. Now, smiling, blowing kisses, carrying her own boxes.

She told me that she was mostly glad that I lied to her: that there was a Santa Claus, that the tooth fairy left the quarter. So, she now loves to help and play with little kids too. "Yes, dad, of course, I want to be a mother."

She has even recently given ME good advice when I am upset. Jaimelyn supports even ME sometimes.

She will marry Andrew, maybe live in the Apt. her mother Karen now has when Karen is gone, and probably raise a little one in the room that was once her's.

Little Jaimelyn into the dorm, out the other side, and…. goes on past me.

I wave. She acknowledges my wave, and blows me another kiss.

18. Yet, how wonderful

I am locked inside here
with only these eyes
and only these ears.

I can only see what *I* see,
what *I* hear.

I can only taste with this tongue
and only touch with these hands.

I have only the drive
of my hopes, and needs and cares.

Yet, how wonderful it is
that I can listen
to how everything is
to someone else's ears,
someone else's eyes, tastes, and touch.

Everyone brings me more eyes and ears,
tastes and touch.

Howard Seeman, Ph.D.

Everyone brings me more hopes and needs
and cares and wants.

All are messengers
come back to me
waiting here in my small place.

One comes now.
I listen.

What more can you bring me?

19. Now realizing I loved

I loved so many but was too young to know it. My realization now comes when I am 74, but then I was only 5, or 8 or 12… I loved them, but now, they are gone, and I can't tell them or hug them. I got smart but now too late to tell them they were great in many ways, and kiss them, and do for them as they did for me…. But, they are gone. Sad. I want to go on top of a mountain with a huge megaphone and tell them: "I loved you, but did not know it." They are in the clouds? Or across an ocean? "I now realize I loved you!" But, they cannot hear me.

I want to wrap a gift for each, in colorful paper, and then watch them open these gifts, and see them put their hands to their hearts and say: "Thank you".

Some of them may even have needed this then, but now it is too late.

-- My dear little friend: Irwin, who died at 13 years old. I thought: he was just a cute friend who I played Monopoly with, who could bite his toe nails, laughed when I tried to make him laugh, and felt sad that he was fat and often picked last for the team when we played stick ball. He did not do anything to warrant getting cancer. He did not even have the chance to be a teenager, wink at girls, have some money of his own – so that he would not have to ask his mother in order to buy baseball cards. It was unfair that he had to go. Little Irwin should not have gone so soon.

--Irwin my dear little friend, here: a hug, a kiss for thee and a small gift for you, since I loved you. Here: a little silver dog you used in order to go around the Monopoly Board. Bye my dear friend. I loved you.

-- Mr. Bryer. I was scared of you. You were the super, the superintendent of our building that yelled at us kids: "Get outa here!" because we were making too much noise in the lobby, or were playing too loud on the sidewalk. You had an accent; that made you scarier.

But, now I realize you were probably upset, you lived in the basement, and had to clean very dirty things down there, and had to live in that no-windows basement apartment; maybe rats, certainly roaches, were there. That is all you could probably afford, you were, now I realize: an immigrant, trying to make it. You must have been under great stress. Sorry I added to your upset. I was little and wanted to just play. For us you were the useful "bad-guy" we could all laugh at.

Sorry. Here, you deserve at least a warm handshake, and: "Sorry I upset you". Hope your family is ok. Hope they grew up better than you had, with more money and less stress....now, especially that you are gone. Sorry Mr. Bryer. Here is a gift: I brought you and your family some Dixie ice cream cups, and a little card: "Thanks for helping our building be our home." Love, Howard

-- Elliot, Cliffy, little Michael, all those kids playing Potsy on the sidewalk. I should have, wish I could have, loved you. I now realize you were all more than just cute kid-friends that I played with. You were all not aware that you would grow up to be adults, fear aging, and worry about your kids. You just tried to win points, laugh with each other, and worried you would not be liked, and afraid of, but needing, your mommy and daddy. The cracks on the sidewalk were an important part of your/ our world. Balls bouncing - were our UP as we whiled away our days. We came out onto the street every day worrying that we would not get picked, and played to forget *school...* the road out of our childhood.

Now, I wish I could give you all points, pick you all, tell you that all will be ok for a long while, and help you with your getting older. I can't, couldn't, and I am too. I did love you all.

-- The man who managed that drug store where I got my first job. I don't even know your name. I remember sitting on a stool, waiting and waiting in your drug store. I was probably 12 years old. I just waited there, sometimes even an hour until someone came in and ordered a prescription, and then left. And then about a half hour later, the medicine was ready.

My job? To deliver this medicine to that person. I had to look at the address, get directions, run up those stairs to Davidson Avenue, the block above the drug store, find the correct building, push the correct apt. button number on the directory in the entranceway, be let in, go up the elevator, ring the door bell, and give the medicine to this person.

I got a "thank you" and a tip. Money. My first job: delivery-boy for the pharmacy. Mr. Smith? Mr. Manager of the drug store? Sorry, I do not know your name. You gave me my first job; I think my mother asked you if I could do this job.

Thank you, my first job, the track I had to get on in order to get another job, and then another job…in order to grow up, get money, learn about money [how it can help and hurt]…onward and onward to job, to job… to finally be a teacher and then a college professor. But, it started with me waiting on that stool in your drug store. Thank you Mr. Smith, I would never have been a college professor if it were not for you.

Now I realize: you were not just the manager of the pharmacy, but probably also a dad, and that means you were probably once a little boy too. And you probably had kids and a wife. And, probably they were sometimes a struggle for you, stress you had before you went to work each day in that drug store. Probably, while you gave me my directions of where to deliver the medicine…you also had some other worries on your mind.

So thank you for putting these worries aside for a moment, to explain the address to me, and let me sit there on the stool, to give me my first job.

Here's a hug for you, and if I could find a small trophy of a man bending down to give a little boy a small package, hopefully at least in brass, I would, if I could, [but you are gone] give it to you. Here: with love, Howard

-- Otto. Otto. Even saying his name is emotionally still dear to me. What was almost profound, but you do not think so, was that he made me laugh - and so wonderfully much. Humor, especially warm affectionate humor, is really a 23 letter word, full of side kisses, fast hugs, fur, warmly wrapping its given-tos with winks and care, in order to make them happier.

Otto did this Humor, and often; and he helped me do that too [a secret mutual loving]. *Funny* is a poor word for this kind of loving. *Funny* seems trite, and silly. Silly is certainly too low a word for this wonderful giving. HUMOR-WARM-CARE is this food-medicine, a bonding, a short, fast intimacy, in a package that is easier to take than other intimacies that don't have fur.

Otto gave HUMOR and brought it out in others, for others. And I was one of those who got his caring-laughter cookies.

But the deeper profundity of all of this was: that Otto, while he gave, was also secretly in pain. When he got tired, or when he was resting from running and giving this kind of love [when he was out of energy from shielding his pain] he let me know of what he suffered from, and still suffered from. I had only a peek at this: He told me one day, [we were roommates], that he remembered his 13 year old sister running past him to bathroom. She sat on the toilet, while he heard her crying; a large blood clot came out of her vagina: an unborn fetus. She had finally miscarried after months of hiding and carrying a baby, probably forced into her by a rape.

I could then feel one of Otto's sufferings, this painful remembrance he had with him since he was 15; but this was probably only one of his sufferings. If this could happen with his sister, what kind of other sufferings had this dear Otto gone through? He carried them all. But, now, mostly tried to cover these, heal them with that 23 letter word: HUMOR. Dear Otto, I loved you, I love you.

Now?

I am slowly dying of pancreatic cancer [in months, a year, a couple of years?] I am soon 76 years old. I am on the last downhill of the wonderful roller coaster. But, from having been up here and through all these turns, my view has gotten wider: I now realize that <u>even all the people I do not know</u>, all these people - <u>are also</u>: Irwin, Mr. Bryer, Elliot, Cliffy…, all those kids playing potsy, are all the manager of the drug store, and all Ottos.

If I do not love these strangers, even the ones passing me on the street, it is because I do not realize fast enough that they too are like all the ones I knew.

Love, Howard

20. Longing: where are they?

Where is Linda? Where is Mrs. Morris? Ricky? Larry? Dr. Lauer? And Gene?

They are all inside me, who moved me into my life's directions…but, now, where are they? They are on my shelf? Where is that shelf? Did I leave it in the last apartment I rented? Do they still follow me down the street? Do they talk to each other? Or, are they just a story told by a narrator in a film about my life?

Linda: We roller skated together at 8 years old. Kind of the darlings of Davidson Ave. Then, roller skating together was the 8 year old equivalent of making love, going all the way. She was even more exciting because she was a red head. When she came out of the lobby toward me onto the street, my heart pounded like seeing a sunrise. After about a year of roller skating, and loving each other [though we did not know how to do that], we rode the elevator to the sixth floor, to my Apt. door. My mother opened the door. Linda and I looked at each other, and then we both, with full knowledge and consent, feeling we were now big: 8 years old – told my mother: "Linda and I want to get married." My mother of course just laughed at us, with disrespect. About a year later, a very tall guy [he must have been 10] started to be with Linda instead of me. I lost Linda. Very sad, angry…I wondered how I could get to be that tall, and have big shoulders like that and play ball like him. This depression lasted for years. I still have the longing of it. Where is Linda? Linda! Did you go to college, then meet your husband and then move to England? Do you now have kids, four grandchildren? Are you still pretty? Or are you just sad… and just watch TV? Linda, where are you?

Where is Mrs. Morris? After trying to make my mother since I was two years old into a better loving mother, I met Mrs. Morris when I was 12, when I entered the 7th grade. She winked at us [and me], chewed gum with a smile, played piano for us to sing together – to make us into a family. She cracked cute jokes, but never ones that hurt us; only ones that she could use to give us smiles. When she waved her arms to conduct us singing – they were like hugs. Being with her my loneliness melted. She loved us, and kissed us kids with warm together-music. What happened to her? She had a son: Richie, who sometimes came to our class. How do I become Richie, I wondered? Does she now need anything? I would pick up whatever she dropped and be honored to pick it up first. Then, her smile back would be a gift I could take with me. And, I have.

Mrs. Morris? Are you OK? If not, I want to help. Here, here is your love back. I hope you are not in a nursing home watching TV. Hopefully, you're at a piano…still playing, but now for those old people. Where are you? Please call me. I want to hug you back.

Ricky. Where are you? Do you know that if it were not for you, I probably would have never have been a teacher, my major identity, the rest of my life. Though I wanted to be a teacher since I was 12, when I left my first year of high school – moving with my family out of the city to Lake Mohegan- you were pretty much my only friend. And you lived in the house right behind my house. I arrived at Lake Mohegan High School with a lousy 68 average in my first year of high school, almost failing. Why? I never did my homework. I was a lazy student. However, after school once I moved out of the city, since I had no one to play with but you up there, I went over to your house, and you were always be doing your dam homework. You wanted very much to become an optometrist. At first, each time I came over, I got bored with you doing homework, so I left you. But, eventually, since I had no place else to go…I went to you… and, begrudgingly <u>also</u> did homework with you – for the next 3 years of high school.

By the time I was a senior, my high school average went from a 68 up to an 85, and I started to like being good at school. You Ricky, you; you made me do my homework. I thus was able to get into Albany State University

Teacher's College. Motivated, I did well, and then on to graduate school, a scholarship for my M.A. in philosophy, eventually my Ph.D…. and I have now been a teacher for 51 years. Do you know this? Nah, I don't think you do. You do not even know where I am – but we were close friends for those years in high school. I helped you become a basketball star in high school, feeding you the ball after school in a small playground- so you could practice and practice. Are you an optometrist? Where are you? Hope you are happy. Thank you for doing your homework… and pulling me up with you. Thank you. I miss you.

Larry? Where are you? You seemed always tall and strong, and wise; at least you feigned that well. Do you know that you changed my life when I was 26? Besides feeling brotherly with you, which I never felt till then, you said one day: "Let's go to this workshop on: "Sensitivity Training". No big deal I thought: another workshop. However, there I met Bob Siroka. At this session, a group member talked about his feelings toward his father. I suddenly, while listening, felt water on my hands; I was crying. After this group member finished, Bob leading the group asked: "Anyone share similar feelings?" I started to share that I was also sad about my father. But, Bob interrupted me and said: "I don' think you feel sad; I think you feel ANGRY with your father." That comment hit me hard and then brewed in me upsettingly as I walked home with you Larry that night. After chewing on this comment for days, I finally could feel: Yes, I was ANGRY at my father. I called Bob and went to my first therapy session; that was in 1968. Larry, from that day on…. I have taken, been through, done thousands of hours of therapy and training related to emotional growth. That workshop you had us go to affected all I did when I was a teacher in the high schools, then teaching educational psychology for 30 years as a professor, then my own work therapizing teachers, teaching psychodrama, how I looked for friends, how I coped with my marriage, how I raised my emotionally smart daughter, how I love my loved ones, and how I am…very much today in general. Larry, Lawrence, you did that!

Are **you** ok? I hear you have done good social work things. Great. You did one great one for me. Hope you are well. Thank you for that night's suggestion.

My love, Howard

Dr. Lauer? Professor Lauer, my first philosophy professor. Where are you? Do you still smoke a pipe? I don't think so; when I was 21, 3rd year of college, you were about 60. Now I am 75. However, you live on, having influenced my life. You were *my warm first smart father*. My real father was not smart, nor warm. I had met some smart father figures, who I looked up to, hoping they would look after me. But, none of them did and were not warm. I also had met some warm men, but none were smart enough for me to want to follow them as a substitute father. You were *my warm first smart father*. If I said something smart, you did not put me down or try to better me. You did not feel less if I had a good point. You were one of the first men to help me feel smart. I could also feel your desire to guide me. You took me to my first church meeting. [I had only been to synagogues.] It was a Unitarian Church. To my surprise, the minister there read a literature passage about hatching sea turtles on the beach rushing to get into the ocean – to not be eaten by birds. A sea captain sees this and remarks to a sailor: "I just saw god." This was not the usual God praising sermon, but spoke of life's often brutally and struggle. It was simple and powerful to me. It got me so much, that in the next month or so, I almost decided to become a Unitarian Minister. Dr. Lauer, you also invited us, your students, into your home. That you were almost legally blind, made you even more humble. And you could do that, without being embarrassed or annoyed. I hoped I could do that ability someday too; you gave me that sense of pride at resilience. Thank you for taking me under your wing. I did *think/feel* better from what you gave me, from then on. Thank you Dr. Lauer.

Gene? Where are you? If it weren't for you, I would have married a certain woman and would have been miserable, maybe the rest of my life. In college you noticed [you and I were total strangers] that I went from a guy kidding around … to then into a deep depression while dating this woman. You approached me out of nowhere and told me that you noticed this and you were concerned. A long story, but you pulled me out of this bad relationship. However, now I realize: you had sensitivity, a compassion, and an ability to love – a stranger. You did that toward me; out of nowhere. Then, we became friends for years and years.

Then, after college, I learned you loved the army, and detective magazines, and you had an NRA streak in you? Gene, I don't understand who you became… and now: where you are? I know you had a lousy father;

so did I. Are you OK? Thanks for saving me. I should get back to you, find you, help you too if you need it. I think I will. Gene, I am coming to you; I will find you. Hope you are not as old as I think you may be, as I now am. We should hug and reminisce. Unknowing in many ways… we did feel love and care for each other. I will find you and do for you too if I can.

Love, Howard

21. Serious games

We tell each other about these games we did as kids with a smile on our faces, we even laugh together at the fun we had playing them. But, each of us, almost as a secret, know these games, then, were also "serious", sometimes even scary.

In *Hide and Go Seek,* When "It" started to count to 100 we ran for our lives, because if we were found, we would be killed, or laughed at by all the kids on the block, which was the same thing. We did not stop to realize that we had run to a spot to hide where we were now all alone, maybe for a long year of: 15 minutes, and in the dark! In the dead silence there, we feared if we even moved, "It" might find us! And, if he did, we needed to run for our lives back to the base or god forbid... We would be IT. Then, everybody would run away from us, like we were a disease. When we were IT, and finished counting to 100 and could finally open our eyes... the whole block was totally empty! Our friends had run away from us. No more friends. This was fun?

Do you remember how much money we were supposed to give out when you started playing Monopoly? We could volunteer for this job, but then we ran the risk of someone saying: "No, you idiot, only two $500s." But, we wanted to do this job so much so we could feel some power, at least for a couple of minutes. Then, we all shot the dice, highest went first. I knew we were playing this game just in Eddie's house, but it felt like we were in the stadium of the US Open.

I usually picked the little silver dog, not the tank, or the dumb shoe.

The dog might get me some sympathy, in case I landed on Boardwalk and Park Place.

And, when else in your life would you be glad to get a *Get Out of Jail Free* card? Certainly not in the real mail! Getting around the board and passing GO, was like completing a developmental task for Abraham Maslow. And, when we passed GO, our blood pressure actually came down a little; and we also got $200. Then, in those days, Life was about passing GO? It still is!

When we played Checkers, it did not seem like a game just for 8 year olds in sleep away camp, This game felt like it proved your total life's competence, especially when you got "taken" and you started to run out of checkers. Checkers affected our whole ranking on your block, especially during rainy days. This game smelled like Life. Did we feel that about Checkers? Nah, it was just a game. Nah, Life!

Playing *Spin the Bottle* was like a roller coaster up a skirt, with all those girls with new breasts looking at us. Did we know this was the long road to eventually foreplay, to finally having real sex, and making babies? Having to kiss a girl was great and scary, especially since we had no practice at it, and there was no book on this in the school library. Then, we did NOT kiss as we felt; that took confidence. No one had confidence then. We also knew that when this game was over, all the girls would talk about us, or we hoped so.

When we played basketball, and decided to take that shot, this courageous decision might be seen as self centered, especially if you missed. But, if it went in, maybe you could get points that could help your ranking on the whole block, in your whole childhood… at least for a couple of minutes.

I dreaded that they were organizing a stick-ball game. Why? You would have to stand there while the two captains picked who they wanted on their team. And every time you were not picked, you were more alone. You feared being picked last, in front of everybody, you would be in the "not-picked-dungeon"! You had no therapist for this scar, even your mother would think it no big deal. This *last- picked wound* you would carry around for the next 20 years of your life. This was the upset that stuck in your mind; so that when you eventually became 42, because of this old wound - you joined a Gym.

Going up on the roof, hiding from my parents, to play Poker, though it was just for dimes and nickels – felt like I was able to be in a James Cagney movie, a fugitive from the law among other thieves: I could: GAMBLE! When we played Poker, we suddenly were older; we were no longer 12, but more like 57, and we had a beard, and fancy shoes, though we really were only wearing Keds. And we talked "tough", since all those kids around the table were now also 57. And, we could lie! We could bet high and convince them we had 4 aces, when we really had nothing. This was called Bluffing? Nah, this was: LYING! And we could finally lie and mom and dad could not punish us. Playing Poker was almost permission to be evil. What a breath of fresh air [after walking around all our lives for 12 years] holding all of this mean-ness in. And this game had real MONEY. We sometimes got the thrill of racking in a pile of like 20 dimes and nickels [it made a great sound] and sometimes even large quarters. Then, we maybe could buy not just one thing, but 5 things, at the candy store. But, we could also be *shrunk* to smithereens if we lost all our money: the $2.50 our dad gave us for taking out the garbage. That would be scary: we would have to create an alibi to our dad about where all our money went, and again he might send us to jail without dinner.

I got through all of these games. Did you?

Since *hide and go seek*, I hide less; hiding makes me lonely. Instead, I try to forgive myself, and thus find the courage to tell people what I did, so I am no longer alone in the dark constantly trying to run to find that safe base.

Since playing Monopoly, I can value money less, and have passed enough *Go-s*, with rewards better than getting $200. And, if I lose, I find that by talking to others and myself, I can feel OK again. So, I worry less about losing in general.

Since playing Checkers, I can now play it with no worry that it is about Life. It is now fun getting to all those little squares, better than worrying about the Big Squares in my appointment book.

Since playing *spin the bottle,* I can kiss with honest confidence and follow my feelings, And I have graduated from just kissing, to following/hugging/touching the whole person.

Since worrying about being picked last for a team, I now know ahead of time that I will not get picked first or even 5th, nor score very high on

S.A.T. tests. I have enough things I am good at - such that if not picked, I can just judge my judger or enjoy being part of the game, even if I am number...nine.

Since secretly gambling, I don't do it any longer for need or for scary drama or to be bigger, but for fun. And, I don't need to gamble in secret – since what I am gambling is mine, not my Dad's. Also, I am really now 57, even higher, and don't need to wear fancy shoes nor talk tough.

I have also won some races, made some of my checkers into kings, have the nerve to try difficult shots; and can even strike out, feel sad, but then grow myself back up again.

And, even more important, since doing all of these games, all these games are now...finally, less serious.

22. Sitting by the ocean trying to be great

Don't be (as a wave comes and hits the shore)
ridiculous.
You can't write
sitting by the ocean
trying to be great
writing by the ocean
about the ocean
trying to be great.

Don't be ridiculous.

It's wider than your eyes
sitting by the ocean trying to be great.

What are you crazy?

Do you know how many people stare
have spent days
books full of trying to write waves
sitting by the ocean trying to be great.

What are you kidding?

From Europe it tumbles
and tumbles into canyons
and is alone out there
and doesn't care, noticed or unnoticed
even in the night.

and nowhere does it have eyes
or arms
but all eyes and arms and all arms and eyes;
tumbling from Europe,
all at once
a not man's monster
doing it all (care or not) alone.

I'm no longer sitting by the ocean trying to be great.

It has scared me away.

I'm as all things to it.
I came from it, they came from it.
Somewhere we all remember.

I'm no longer sitting by the ocean trying to be great.

It has taken my talking away.

I'm a piece of cliff
or one day:
but one of the airs in the sky
or
(from Alpha Centori)
no difference.

It's that
all of space and the ocean and the violence of the stars
are too loud to hear.

We are it is all of us are it
space, the ocean,
and I'm gone.

I'm certainly, no longer, certainly
ever sitting by the ocean trying to be great.

23. Learning/Talking to the Sunrise at the Cliffs

I grew up in the Bronx on a block. Up and down the street were just big apartment buildings and parked cars. All my life I had only seen the sun mid-afternoons peak out from behind high buildings - Never seeing the sun as THE SUN out there in space, an actual star throwing light onto this planet where I lived. I had a narrow perspective. This bright yellow ball that only hung above buildings in the afternoons – was only that: a bright yellow ball– and, thus, I was only a kid on a block, where sometimes the sun came out. And there was no other "real place" besides this block, my block.

I also never saw this sun go down. It only just slowly went behind buildings, as the day went on, and then it just got darker on my block.

However, years later when I was 24, a woman invited me to Cape Cod with some friends that had a small cottage near a cliff that overlooked the ocean. She casually suggested that I get up early the next morning to watch the sunrise; "It's a nice view from here". She did not know that I had never seen a sunrise.

So the next morning, alone, I got up at 5:30am and, wrapped in a blanket, sat down at the edge of these cliffs to see my first sunrise. Again, I had never seen the sun, itself, rise, come up toward me, me sitting on this planet.

Finally, after waiting, with some suspense, about 5:45am…. it happened, it protruded, started to rise. It rose slowly, out of the whole ocean far away on the horizon!

It changed me forever!

I don't understand this sunrise

I don't understand this sunrise
from this cliff.

I don't understand this parade-all-by-itself,
climbing;
that nothing lifts it
from such wide all-shoulders Ocean.

I don't understand this sunrise
from this alone, all the way over here.
How, Why it comes out of the ocean there,
no sound?

How can there be
carburetors
and computers,
or how can I be
back hustling my alarm clock
and get voice mail
in a room with walls.

How is there such a roar I can't hear?
And why don't the waters there
where it comes
rise up, surge-bewondered,
and rush-in-a-crowd?

Why does not this cliff
explode now
and fly?

And this piddling-with-my-face-wind
stop
take on eyes
and gape?

Why does not this darkness of
light years of night sky, moon and stars
refuse

such a Universe Buzz Saw
burning,
rolling across?

Why am I suddenly afraid it may have eyes?
Why am I suddenly but a piece of cliff,
a non-member, lost midst
The Gathering of God's Control-Room?

I don't remember any appointment here.
Am I supposed to do something?

I don't understand.
I don't understand this sunrise.

The sunrise again

I came to see this almost 12 years ago.
Then, it was my first.

This time I took the car road there
and went to see: What now? How is it now?

(and the fear I knew that it was about me.)

This time I was bothered with
the cold wind,
being on time,
and trying to focus.

I had to tell myself:
this is it, be here!

I was, but differently.

It was a panoramic scene.
And, the ocean's waves below were friendly
(I'd been in them.)

This time the cliffs were not after me,
nor there a million years before me.
(they were)
but they were also here now;
with no evil in them that might get me.

Then, I looked for it:

The Sun.

I was ready to be scared.

I was alone, over fragilely the open ocean.

I was alone in my life here,
to feel my life alone.

I was about to see,
without any permission,
the birth of a star.

I was here to decide who I had become.

There was a kind of a drum roll,
but with cotton brushes.

It shocking-wondered me how such a thing could do that.

But as it grabbed over the oceaned horizon,
far off from my windy cliff,
(though it's light was amazing,
the source of all life)
It was OK.

No thorn was in the light;
no fear did it put on me;

It was just doing its thing
grandly.

I didn't need to hold onto myself for protection.

It was the sun and me.

Each by ourselves.

And it didn't mind.

I watched it take off all it's clothes,

and its earth.

It was not angry at me.
(Giants never fear
thus never need anger.)

The sun's rise was g l o r i o u s l y;
as it should be.
And I was ordinary,
as I should be.

I could've gotten into my car and left at any time
but I waited.

"Where's that grand scary part?" I asked.

It never came.

It's just the sun.

It's just
me watching the sunrise,

and then …

home.

Howard Seeman, Ph.D.

I am at the cliffs again

I am at the cliffs again.

Fifteen years ago, I decided I was born here.

And now I'm at the cliffs again.

The only person it seems
that is still with me
through graduations,
remembering when I was thirteen,
and getting more serious about growing older
is me.

I'm at the cliffs again.

Much has changed inside me:
I tend to remember
the ocean much less.
But, thankfully,
the ocean still remembers me,
knows I'm here –
though I only matter
as much as this cliff.

I'm at the cliffs again.

Much has died behind me;
a funeral parade I have slowly come by to be here.

No more Leona.
She's gone my dear cliffs;
don't know where.
If I ever see her,
I'll send her your regards.

No more Gene
my dear cliffs.
He's gotten older and
plays ball to pretend young,
because he's lost and doesn't know where to find them.
And that's all he's been.
Sad, my dear cliffs.

No more parents; they have died.
They got older
my dear cliffs,
were also children trying to be for each other.
They are now in <u>my</u> photo album.

No more: "I don't know how," my dear cliffs.
I'm grown-up.
I know *how* many things now.
Waiting to learn for someone has to show me,
is over.

I'm now the one who shows;
I'm a father and an uncle;
there are more little ones around me
than big ones.

I'm at the cliffs again.

I'm so glad you still recognize me.
I want you to know I will keep coming back
to you.
I did when I was 35,
then 40, then 60
and now when I am old, being soon over,
sadder and slower,
and soon will need help to get here.

I'll be coming here.
Keep a place for me.
I'll write my last to you, I promise.

And then you and they can throw it to the wind.
Kiss a wave goodbye to a ship,
and be off
to spend your next light years,
sunrises, ocean, and other travelers
at the cliffs again.

Again at the cliffs

No need any longer to capture
at the cliffs again.

They'll be here, and I can go elsewhere.

My home is now almost all inside me,
with those I love,
and with the knowledge I can....

I no longer need to capture, go to, every year,
being at the cliffs again.

This monster SUN, as it every day takes its seat in the sky, now looks familiar, getting smaller and smaller as it rises, looks more like my old yellow ball that I saw behind the buildings when I was a kid.

I can now see that this SUN was the same sun. That it is not a stranger, it knows me, and I know IT. It's just those days again, but now different from on my block and being a little kid. Now, I understand it.

My block was my narrow world. But now I understand it was not just a block, but in a city, on a continent, on a planet going around a star. Perhaps other worlds are doing the same? I realize that, although I am just a piece of cliff, I am privileged, am alive to witness it all, honored.

And I notice that all of this is in *time*, not just the hands on my clock....but the time of billions of years before I was a kid.... And billions of years before that.....and will go on billions of years after I am no longer here.

From that sunrise on that day, from that event, finally, surly, I cannot avoid that I am mortal; I will surly die someday. But, with that sunrise....I now KNOW all this.

As this familiar sun now takes its normal place in the sky, it no longer looks monstrous, but friendly- I am now a "member" of the cliffs.

Even the cliffs accept me. I have permission to see again, and again this grand becoming everyday.

The sunrise is now not scary; it is just: *Glorious!*

I can lie back in my living room,
or just watch Jaimelyn,
[and can even die, if I have to, not at the cliffs, but home.]

Cliffs, we'll always be friends,
I just may not need to call on you anymore.

24. When I was eight years old

When I was eight years old,
I was sure I could fly
if I jumped off a roof
and did not get scared
and just kept believing
I would not fall.

Today, I don't even have the omnipotence
to not get fatter.

I am really now convinced that
no matter how hard I try
there are many, many things
I (no matter how much I believe,
jump, want, think I can)
can't do.

I also did not talk like this when I was eight years old.

Many things now remind me of
looking out the rear window of a car:

My daughter is now where I once was.
Sometimes she looks at me as I will have been to her
when she no longer needs me.

Howard Seeman, Ph.D.

When she turns away to go to play,
I see that
she is already
a sunset memory I will have.

I see the seasons change
and now remember
how easily it happens.

There are much fewer new things.

I see the beginnings of things
that I will not see finish.

Sometimes I catch myself
(with a fear that I quickly rush by)
that when I am planning,
it makes no sense to figure that far.

Next, I will have to accept
that it's not that I did not get enough sleep,
nor ate wrong,
or need more exercise.

25. Glad you helped me climb up out of it

You each filled in little holes in me, soothed my old bleedings, hugged my pains to calm, held my hand, reached for it - so that I could climb up out of my childhood damages. Little things you did helped:

- Mr. Briar, the super of our building, who usually was always yelling at us kids, actually winked at me one day when I was about 5, a kind of: "Hi ☺" This scary man was nice to me! He liked me for a second, rather than yelled at me. That little *syrup* went in.
- Carol, that girl I enamored-over in 3rd grade, I think was not rejecting my smiles at her? Maybe she even liked me? Maybe, I felt then: I am not so unlikable?
- Irwin, Eddie, Arthur, Lloyd… so glad you laughed when I made jokes. I did have to, want to, try hard at these. I needed the drink of others' smiles at me. You started to make me feel like I could be good at something.
- Leona: you did not say: "I don't want this." when I gave you that silver dollar I cut in half for you. Thank you. I would have been devastated…still. You, in a way told me, "You're not so bad."
- Mrs. Morris, my chorus teacher: thanks for being my best first mother, and giving me *together singing,* a wanting I would seek then for the rest of my life.
- Larry: That you were tall and spoke that way sounding wise; you felt like my friend-big brother. That made me feel safer. Thank you.

- Mr. Greenstein: a male teacher who laughed with me, cared about me – and did it like a real person, even had a girlfriend, like a real person. I was almost, for often minutes: your "son", or at least your "nephew".

- Thank you Mr. Davis, my high school English teacher. I thought you were only teaching us some poetry, but this made me reach inside with this new *flash light*, finding some smoldering hurt-meS in there that I began to write about and eventually well, and better and better. You gave me the tool-voice I now use to connect with others and make them more aware: my ability to write poetry.

- Ricky, my friend across my backyard all through high school: for [not just making me do homework] but also for sometimes squeezing my arm with affection – I knew you had to be comical when you did that; affection for us, for you, was embarrassing.

- My first philosophy professor: Dr. Leau: You listened to me as though my comments were smart, and as I went on in "philosophy"…I found out [from my having to introspect so much of my pains when I was a little boy] I was! You led me down the road of noticing my insides, if only then mostly in thoughts. But, hidden in those idea-labyrinths were: loneliness, fear of dying, suppressed hurt and anger… Eventually your support of my thinking/exploring was the start of noticing and expressing my feelings - then tangled onlyd in my "analyzing epistemology."

- Robert, my dear Bob, Siroka: You helped me find my-feeling channel, my emotional underground stream running in my cave river: my feelings. At the end of my first therapy session, I asked: "Well, what do you think?" You said with care-directness [that I would then trust for the next 49 years]: "You are intellectually smart but emotionally retarded." You taught me how to identify my feelings, trust them, feel unalone about them, even ugly ones became just naturally human. You taught me how to feel real connected intimacy, less fear of anger, and courage/pride about my vulnerabilities. You listened soothingly, taught me how to work on feeling good about myself [more important than "winning"], how to mine the *gold* in really listening, and accepted all of me to boost that I was worthy, very capable and loveable. You helped me build this now *me*, eventually to the special icing on the cake: that loving is even more fulfilling than being loved. <u>*A lesson here:*</u>

The story goes that two hikers, both strangers to each other, are hiking alongside each other, and they stop at a small stand along the empty route to buy a drink. As one of them reaches into his pocket to pay, the other notices a small beautiful precious stone mixed with the man's money. The other exclaims: "What a beautiful stone that is!" The other responds: "Thank you. Yes. ..... Do you want it?"

"Me? Want it? But, it's yours!" "Yes, but if you really like it so much.... here!" And the man gives him the stone. "Sorry, I have to go now, enjoy the stone." And the man walks on ahead. The man given the stone is flabbergasted. He feels this gift ...and thinks and thinks Finally, he runs up ahead to catch the man who gave him the stone: "Thank you so much, but here, please take back the stone; I don't want the stone..... What I want is: what you have to be able to give me the stone."

Apropos: I once told Bob Siroka: "Thank you so much for your care and help." He replied: "Nah, I just do it for the money."

You helped me build the now me that is good-caring about others often without even thinking about it. You helped me feel even good enough that, if I die, even soon, I will not have anger with my dying, but *a-proud-of-my-life*: the best final accomplishment.

- Karen: For pushing me to have a child that gave me: doing greater loving, more fulfilling than being loved. And, for doing the best you could do with your own childhood with us, while doing your best to handle my childhood.

- Lynda Wismer: For modeling the best attitude about aging. Once when Lynda babysat Jaime-lyn [named after this <u>Lynda</u>], she played a game with her: "Jaimelyn, let's both sit in rocking chairs and talk to each other as if we are both now old ladies." Jaimelyn was 8 years old then. Lynda was 76.

- My dear daughter Jaimelyn: Nietzsche said that: "Of all the illnesses, keep *not-caring* farthest from me." Well, JJ, my dear, your *just being*, no matter what you do, - makes all I do, see, want, and feel all of my life...the complete opposite of that illness.

- Dan: For letting me ride sidecar with you, and you riding sidecar with me... for over 43 years.
- Ron/Debra: For giving me an oasis to get away to where I can re-drink our past and pet [and she pet me]: Dusty.
- Steve: For listening to me so well, for giving me you, and allowing me to be one of the few you tell to; for comforting so many of my anxieties, and the bonding of our laughing and caring for each other for over 25 years.
- Brenda: For your openness and honesty with me, and being there for each other for over 44 years.
- Ros: For convincing me, [by our being with each other, and by your total honesty no matter what] that I am loveable.
- Sherry: For finding me. For being you – that ignites again in me: my loving, my care, respect, humor and protecting- that I love feeling.
- And thank you to all my friends and family who let me in on your tender private feelings. Such honors me, allows me to help, helps takes away my aloneness and makes my life feel valuable. *Caring-Giving-Attachments* are the highest use of my being alive.

I am locked inside here with only these eyes and only these ears. I can only see what I see, what I hear. I can only taste with this tongue and only touch with these hands. I have only the drive of my hopes, and needs and cares.

Yet, how wonderful it is that I can listen to how everything is to someone else's ears someone else's eyes, tastes, and touch. Everyone brings me more eyes and ears, tastes and touch. Everyone brings me more hopes and needs and cares and wants. All are messengers come back to me waiting here in my small place. One comes now. I listen. What more can you bring me?

26. Leaving the party

It soon will be my time to have to leave this great party.

For a while there I did not even realize that it was an honor
that I could even be there.

Then, I realized it,
especially when I saw others couldn't stay.

When I remembered this,
[sometimes I did not remember]
I would try to not waste my time there.

I would listen to people well,
eat all the good food I could,
[while not eating too much food
that would have me leaving the party early]

Danced close with people,
seeing them [and me] in their eyes,
and comforted many.

[Sometimes when I petted a dog,
I was not sure if it was the dog or I that was being petted.]

Some people upset at this party would come to me.

Being good to those
was much better than eating all that food.

I can look around the room and feel many ties to them,
and them to each other, and some because of me. I did that.

I am not alone at this party. Thus, I can leave here more easily.

They will all stop for a while,
and wave me a thankful goodbye.

This makes it easier for me to leave.

Glad that I could even be to this party.

A privilege.

27. My last downhill of the roller coaster

What a privilege I have had. This table my computer is on does not feel a thing. I do, and plenty. There are over 300 billion stars in our Milky Way galaxy, and hundreds of billions of other galaxies; they do not *feel* or *know* anything. I do. They are not alive. I am. I see millions of colors, sounds; can taste, touch and reach… whenever I wish. I can see into the eyes of another human being and can feel him/her. I am in a torrent of moving masses, 186,000 miles per second. And am unlike the other trillions of masses, unlike almost everything in the universe, and I know it. I am lit up for this short time with the awesome experience of being conscious. Aware-existence shines through me; I light up all around me. I am an aware-window. What an amazing privilege.

[Besides …being able to taste strawberry short cake, tickle and be tickled, be sexual, swim and float in warm water, play with blocks, watch Laurel & Hardy movies, Daffy Duck cartoons, eat ice cream, play charades, dress up for Halloween, take trips, make camp fires: eat hot dogs, roast marshmallows, sing songs, tell scary stories; go on a zip line, see a parade from dad's shoulders, get a massage, take a hot bath with classical music playing, walk on the beach with the ocean running into your toes, see the starry sky at night from the beach or on top of a mountain, with someone you care about, do an unexpected kiss, reach for their hand….]

Luckily sophisticated chemistry happened to me and made me. But almost not. My parents did not intend to create me. I am alive only due to their need for each other and their sexual attraction. I almost did not become alive. When my mother, who was only nineteen, realized she was pregnant - with fear of little parental support, with the assistance of my father, tried to abort me... by jumping off tables, running in her ninth month, and taking hot baths. I was barely born, premature, turned the wrong way, bleeding, and delivered by forceps.

I will be alive for only a short time more. I am doing a math that I never did before. I remember reading that the new World Trade Center will be finished in about ten years. I stopped to figure it out. Will I see it? I was 62. 62+10 =72. "Yes, probably." I was glad they were building a new park. I was excited that they are building a space station. But, when I heard about plans to land on Mars, I was sad. I will never see it.

I walk by men working on the foundation of a building. All the workers digging in, noisy trucks, dust flying.... I keep walking by; the building's sounds fade. Many of these have all happened before me. Some are now. And some I will never see. Once these were slaves building the Pyramids. They are gone now. This is my time. Now, the noise here is the last movement of a Great Symphony.

In Thorton Wilder's: "Our Town", Emily, who has just died, watches her own funeral and wants to go back to re-experience her 12th birthday. She does, and has a painful realization: "It goes too fast. Live people don't understand."

Our lives move too fast. We realize each week, *that last week was wonderful.* We did the laundry, fixed the faucet, did our checkbook.... But we could've seen the stars, felt the look of a child, and noticed that our hands and feet move and everything else. We realize each week, after that week is over, that last week was wonderful. When we step down, we put an escalator under our feet.

Life is a climb. But, as you come down, you can spread your arms and take all into the appreciation of the climb, past the complaints, the remembrances of the places you've been, feel the privilege you were even allowed to start up this mountain.

You can feel you were and still are being-in-the-world. You can see and feel and hear and taste and touch all the things *that cannot see, feel, hear, taste, or touch.* You can feel like crying from joy or pain, like raging, like caring, hoping, hating, loving, craving; feel sad, mad, bad, glad, clad and had.

Anna Quindlen is said to have reported this realization:

I found one of my best teachers on the boardwalk at Coney Island. He was homeless, and I sat on the edge of the wooden supports with him, dangling our feet over the side. He told me about his schedule, panhandling, sleeping in a church.… But he told me that most of the time he stayed on the boardwalk, facing the water.… And I asked him why. Why didn't he go to one of the shelters? Why didn't he check himself into the hospital for detox? And he just stared out at the ocean and said, "Look at the view, young lady. Look at the view." And every day, in some little way, I try to do what he said. I try to look at the view.

This is my real Final Exam: To do this living/dying well – not pull anyone down as go, widen others, leave red carpets, light, some portable me. I want to be brave: feel <u>every</u> experience, be it pain, fear, sadness… not hold up my arm in front of me to block the winds of these feelings.

I want to understand everyone so well that I cannot be angry with them. I want to accept what others have given me and not be annoyed they did not give more; they did the best they could do.

I now see what is important to do with this life, to keep doing it as much as I can;

to cherish this final living as the thrill of the last downhill of the roller coaster.

DISCOUNT COPIES OF THIS BOOK AND PROF. SEEMAN'S OTHER BOOKS:

THIS BOOK:

❖ Prof. Seeman is available for **Readings and Workshops** on *Personal Creative-Writing: Poetry/Memoirs* for community centers, adult education, nursing homes, retirement residences, small theatres. Participants learn how to do this kind of writing, share with others to form a supportive community, [that can become ongoing], and how to publish these. Fee: $18 [$12/each if you bring a friend]. At these events, Prof. Seeman's books are available at 25% discount. **Interested?** Email Prof. Seeman where such an event near you may be held: ProfSeeman@gmail.com

Author Signed Copies With A Personal Note to You:

One copy: $18   Two: $34   Three: $48   Four: $56

Add $2/bk. for shipping: *SEND TO:*_____

I want___copies.   _____zip_____

Please write this personal note into the book[s]: _____

Send above via email to: **ProfSeeman@gmail.com**

Send $ Total via Paypal to: **ProfSeeman@gmail.com**

"Yes, I may be interested in Prof. Seeman doing a talk/workshop for _____."

- **From Author House:** Authorhouse.com
- **Google:** *Amazon.com:books*

HIS POETRY BOOK:

AT: www.Unlike-Almost-Everything-Else-Universe, Amazon

Have you ever felt so busy that you hardly hear the ocean? Like you are mainly postpone? That your life is just DoingMyLaundry? That you are a place that nobody no longer visits? Then read these poems and feel this restorative call: *Come on, come on, the grand parade is passing right outside your door.* The italicized are just some of the lines from this book of poetry that awaken us to *our awesome privilege of being alive, unlike almost everything else in the universe, as we are lit up for such a short time.* Unfortunately, we may only have these realizations at a funeral, or when we stand on the beach alone at night looking at the stars. But with this book magically *come these precious birds into our hands, these poems: intimate creations, smoldering, precious awakenings.* We can feel a compass in these formed words, Howard Seeman's poetry. Simply keep this wonderful book of poetry near you when you cannot get to the ocean.

<u>HIS EDUCATION BOOKS</u> that emphasize social-emotional learning:

Google: **Seeman, Preventing Disruptive Education, Amazon**

**Prof. Seeman is available at: <u>www.
ClassroomManagementOnline.com</u>
and
Available as a Life-Coach Consultant at: <u>http://
www.echponline.com/bio.html</u>**

Acknowlegements

I wish to thank:

- Carmen Mason, coordinator of Writing My Story at The institute of Retired Professionals at The New School, first motivated me to write these pieces. Writing them felt like hanging out my laundry on a longer line than my poetry had allowed. Her honest critiques and ability to attract astute class members provided useful feedback for me. She supported me midst taking care of personal pressures and the lives of so many others, as she has done for decades.
- Dear Sherry Fine for her support on this project, and her hours of listening/understanding of these and me- that reassured me that these Memoirs were valuably impactful for others.
- Daniela Gioseffi, whose listening and editing suggestions [and her own writing] are so right-on. To have her care to evaluate these memoirs - was a wonderful gift; as it was/is to spend time with her.
- My friends and family for letting me read many of these to you that often helped me validate the worth of these and sometimes notice that they warranted further editing.
- To my dear old friend now gone: Dr. Albert Cullum, who, like Sherry Fine, reinvigorates our care for the children inside all adults. I dedicated my first education book [amazon.com/Preventing-Discipline-Problems-K-12] to: "*To Dr. Albert Cullum, who all too well understood the pains and vulnerabilities of childhood and thus was able to heal so many.*"
- Howard Bruckner, MD., my oncologist [and the staff he fathers] for giving me more life, so I can do more giving with it - that is so fulfilling - that he does with his.

About The Author

Howard Seeman is Professor Emeritus, City University of New York, where he taught educational psychology, group dynamics and human relations 1970 -2000. He is a Certified Life Coach, with a private practice in Jersey City, N.J. and NYC. *At: ProfSeeman@gmail.com* ; Google: *ProfSeemanBio* and an education consultant to troubled teachers at: www. ClassroomManagementOnline.com [that uses his three books in education and over 20 published articles actively, confidentially online.] He is also certified in *The Training of School Violence Prevention and Intervention*. He earned an M.A. and Ph.D. [philosophy, epistemology, social psychology] at the New School for Social Research, NYC, 1970 and 1981; was a Certified, Licensed Teacher of Social Studies and English in High School & Middle School, NYC.

He was/is a member of: The Association for Poetry Therapy; The Association for Specialists in Group Work; The American Association for Counseling & Development; The American Society of Group Psychotherapy and Psychodrama [awarded the title: "Fellow" for his outstanding work in this field]; The Columbia University Seminar on Innovation in Education.

Howard was also an adjunct psychotherapist and led support groups with Dr. Dan Wiener and Dr. Karen Beatty under NYAPS (New York Associates for Psychotherapy Services) in the early 1980s, and taught a Study Group on: *Emotional Intelligence; E.Q. not just I.Q.* [2016] at the Institute for Retired Professionals, New School for Social Research, NYC.

He has been writing poetry since 1958, published his *existential* poems in his book: "Unlike Almost Everything Else in the Universe" [Author/House, 2007]; and also in local journals. He also led poetry support groups for over fifteen years, and has been a reader of his poetry at many bookstores and art venues. Influenced by E. E. Cummings and phenomenologists, Howard's creative writing depicts how experiences honestly present themselves, rather than heeding the rules of language that can distort the accurate descriptive expression of these intimate, *lived*-experiences. Thus, for Howard: being congruent/authentic [as Carl Rogers advocated] is a major value-guideline.

Howard is available for workshops/readings at: <u>ProfSeeman@ gmail.com</u>

Printed in the United States
By Bookmasters